Praise for
My Big Fat Greek Cookb

"Christos has captured the essence of Greek home cooking through this collection of his mother's recipes. An easy-to-read cookbook, emphasizing the simplistic beauty of Greek cuisine."

—Peter Minaki, author of *The Big Book of Mediterranean Recipes*

"Bravo, Christos. Documenting the treasure trove of recipes in a Greek kitchen isn't easy, but it's well worth the effort. I can't wait to pull up a chair and join the feast!"

—Marisa Churchill, *Top Chef* competitor and author of *Sweet & Skinny*

"This cookbook is as much about love as it is about food. A love for family, a love for Greek food, and most of all, a love for the author's mother, who expressed her affection for friends and family through her cooking. Food was her language of love, her recipes preserved for all time in this touching tribute."

—JB Macatulad, willflyforfood.net

"Christos shows us how to make healthy and nutritious recipes, including plant-based meals, and quite honestly inspires us all to own our culture and heritage. Greek cuisine is such a pow-erful way of eating and surely this book will transform us all."

—Maria Koutsogiannis, food stylist, recipe creator, photographer and writer for FoodByMaria

"Who doesn't love Greek food? Years ago, I was invited to Greece to write an article about its cuisine and I had the privilege to stay with a local Greek family. Within five minutes upon my arrival, I was instantly transformed from journalist to family member, and I couldn't stop eating because everything tasted so good! And that family's sense of generosity and pride came rushing back to me when I read Christos's family recipes and memories. The Greeks are masters of simple, accessible, and delicious food. I wish Christos's mother would invite me over to try her yummy galaktoboureko—sweet and crunchy on the outside, and filled with the perfect custard on the inside!"

—Ricardo Larrivée, chef and owner of Cafe Ricardo, host of *Ricardo and Friends* (Food Network), and author of *Vegetables First*

My Big Fat
GREEK COOKBOOK

My Big Fat
GREEK COOKBOOK

Classic Mediterranean Comfort Food Recipes

Christos Sourligas
Recipes by Evdokia Antginas

Foreword by Angelo Tsarouchas

Skyhorse Publishing

Skyhorse Publishing books may be purchased in bulk at special discounts for sales promotion, corporate gifts, fund-raising, or educational purposes. Special editions can also be created to specifications. For details, contact the Special Sales Department, Skyhorse Publishing, 307 West 36th Street, 11th Floor, New York, NY 10018 or info@skyhorsepublishing.com.

Skyhorse® and Skyhorse Publishing® are registered trademarks of Skyhorse Publishing, Inc.®, a Delaware corporation.

Visit our website at www.skyhorsepublishing.com.

10 9 8 7 6 5 4 3 2 1

Library of Congress Cataloging-in-Publication Data is available on file.

Recipes prepared by Evdokia Antginas, Alexandros Sourligas, and Lambrini Sourligas
Photos by Christos Sourligas
Styling by Lambrini Sourligas and Christos Sourligas
Graphic Design Consultant and Photo Editor Nathalie Savoie
Editors: Natalie Karneef and Nicole Frail
Text Review Alex Roslin and Alison Reid
Cover and Additional Photos: Food and Prop Styling by Kerrie Ahern
Cover design by Laura Klynstra
Cover Photography and Additional Photos by Alison Slattery

Paperback ISBN: 978-1-5107-7467-4
Ebook ISBN: 978-1-5107-4985-6

Printed in China

For my sweet, giving, and dedicated Greek Mama, who would do anything for her family.
May your cooking prowess and legacy live for eternity . . .

Contents

Foreword

I first met Christos Sourligas twenty years ago and found him to be a fascinating person. We shared many interests, he being a filmmaker from Montreal, and me starting off in the world of comedy, both of Greek immigrant parents, and the understanding we had growing up in that environment. Especially in the fabled, working-class neighborhood we know as Park Extension. Like most children of immigrants, we quickly had to learn how to adapt to our new country. But the stubbornness of our parents to eat and speak Greek at home could never be challenged.

My Big Fat Greek Cookbook is not only a tribute to Christos's wonderful mama and her yummy passed-down-from-generations recipes, but to all of us in the Greek diaspora who can easily connect to these amazing meals and what it means to them. When the "xeno" (*other*) kids at lunch we're eating PB&Js, we were having moussaka and dolmades as a snack! The recipes in this cookbook not only represent some of the tastiest culinary dishes you will ever eat, but also the love and the passion and the survival of what our parents went through to create a better life for us all.

A lot of my favorite dishes are in this book. And for anyone who has never enjoyed the Greek food experienced before, this is a must-have! It will appeal to every taste bud. And as I browse through it, I can't help but smile at all the memories and holidays each recipe represents for me and for the millions of other fellow members of the Greek community as we were growing up.

It was an honor to write these opening words to commemorate Christos's mother and to keep these fantastic recipes alive for generations to come. I can't wait to prepare some of these dishes with my family. You do us all proud Christos, and your mama, just like mine, will always know that.

—Angelo Tsarouchas, comedian,
actor, lover of food

Introduction

"Your mother has twelve to eighteen months to live."

As soon as the doctors gave my sister and me the news, my mind went into overdrive. *Does Mama have her will in order? What funeral home is best to make arrangements? And when I drive Mama home after her doctor's appointment, what's for dinner?*

But the last thing came first: being the typical filmmaker and storyteller that I am, I needed to document my Mama's Greek food recipes before she passed on. Not because I was going to miss her cooking—although I would, more than I could ever imagine—but because I had to honor this woman while she was still alive by preserving her priceless recipes so that generations to come could savor her life's flavors. The idea being that—say five hundred years from now—someone will pick up this cookbook and make some of my Mama's delicious recipes. This cookbook is bigger than her and me. It's our family's gift to the world. And *that* can never be final.

So, for one year I braved a series of intense hands-on cooking demos with her, my Baba, and my sister to capture an oral history of her gastronomical treasure trove, and I took some abuse along the way: "Teaspoon? What teaspoon? I go with my gut! Back off and just watch me, kiddo!"

And yes, my Mama hung in there until the first edition of her cookbook was released like the stubborn, old-school Greek Mama that she was. She got to see her recipes published and her cookbook adorning bookshelves in stores. Unfortunately, our dear mother passed away about a year after the cookbook's release. It was the hardest thing in the world for me and for my family to deal with, but we're delighted and proud to say that my mom got to witness her success. In fact, the cookbook keeps selling out! Now in multiple editions, her recipes have been proven to be stellar.

Speaking about love and family, "I love you, my son," never rolled off Mama's tongue because she just wasn't brought up to express herself that way. But her succulent comfort food, prepared with such unwavering focus, spoke volumes. This cookbook is a testament to the meme of food as *love*: feeding her family—my Baba, my three siblings, and me, the youngest—was the most meaningful way Mama conveyed her devotion to us. This cookbook is my love letter to her for the sacrifices she made to give her children the life she never had.

My mother posing in her garden as a young lady.

My brother Giannis and Mama lighting candles at church. I just loved her stylish outfits!

Despite growing up in abject poverty, Mama developed a wickedly beautiful and unusual connection to food. During the Nazi occupation of Greece from 1941 to '44, she and her birth family assisted the local Greek resistance fighters by delivering home-cooked meals to their mountain hideouts. And after the war, she and her younger sister Dina traveled the country toiling on factory farms, sending all their measly earnings back home to feed her destitute family. Mama grew up quickly into a bold and sly woman, dubbed "the Spitfire" by friends and family alike.

My Baba, on the other hand, being the loveable conservative man he is, always tried to burst my Mama's bubble by quickly sending their dinner guests on their way well before dessert was even served. Unlike Mama, who always thrived on entertaining, my Baba just didn't like investing the effort to cook for others, nor the noise and laughter that goes with it. Probably because he owned a couple of restaurants himself, so that really zapped any

My baptismal day! I was five years old—unusual for a Greek Orthodox child. Late bloomers rule!

My mama's Greek identity card before she moved to North America.

real love for cooking he ever had. And I can't blame him. They were an adorable, yet oddly mismatched couple. But it worked! She was always a funny bird, my Mama. One of a kind.

As a matter of fact, my siblings and I learned our mischievous ways from my Greek Mama. Like the time on Devil's Night (Montreal, October 30, 1982) when she bought us dozens of fresh eggs from the local grocer so we could toss them on our neighbor's house, who she despised. A liberal at heart, she was extremely open-minded, which completely contrasted her Greek Orthodox religious fervor. So no matter what color, creed, or sexual orientation, she welcomed strangers into her home from all walks of life, and more importantly, she never judged anyone. Why? She simply lived for kitchen-table visits from hungry guests just for the pleasure of seeing them stuff their bellies with her exceptional fare until they couldn't eat another bite.

Now, *My Big Fat Greek Cookbook* is the antithesis of those trendy Mediterranean diets, because most Greeks simply don't eat that way. And certainly not the Greeks of the diaspora, which numbers more than 10 million people. We were brought up eating meat, stewed veggies, potatoes—big, hearty, simple meals from ingredients that my Mama grew or raised herself. Freshness and intense flavor are key in this book. Those qualities Mama knew well and loved, and was the basis of what she prepared for us as a family, wanting her kids to grow up "healthy and strong" as she had.

My brother George and my mother chilling on the porch of our childhood home. Check out those late seventies stylings.

Her recipes are what I call "legit rustic mountain village peasant food." My family is from Arcadia, Greece, and that's what we're highlighting here: the life of the simple shepherd. It's the life idealized by Romantic poets like Lord Byron, Shelley, Keats. Nature. Pasture. Utopia. Where the wilderness is unspoiled and the mountainous landscape so vast, it forces you to connect with the bounty that is . . . *life*. Not a single resident of my Baba's town has ever died of cancer, nor of heart disease. If you walk through the town's cemetery, the average age of death is ninety-five. It's extremely isolated. The mountain roads are treacherous. Cell service is difficult, Wi-Fi nonexistent. And the friends I bring along for my yearly summer visits

My Mama and her uncle, Christos Antginas, who became the family's patriarch after my mother's dad passed away. They were close, as you can see by the smile on my Mama's face.

never want to leave. This is exactly the feeling and emotion my family and I have captured in this book.

As you read through the cookbook, you will come across photos nestled between chapter breaks, all of which I took in and around my mother's village of Nea Chora in the mountainous region of Arcadia, Greece.

So pull up a dining chair and join me on my journey sharing all of my Mama's delicious recipes while bringing to light the real food history of the Greek working class. And as Arcadia is known to be "a land flowing with milk and honey," it's rather fitting that a quarter of my mother's recipes are dedicated to desserts. Mama sure had a sweet tooth!

Bon appétit! Kali Orexi! Opa!
[INSERT the sound of breaking plates here . . .]

Thank you for reading!
All my love,
Christos Sourligas

Monastery of Saint John the Baptist (tenth century) nestled high up on the mountains near my mother's village. Of particular note, her family previously owned and farmed a mountainside next to the monastery.

APPETIZERS

MEATBALLS (keftedes) | 3

PUMPKIN FRITTERS (kolokythokeftedes) | 4

STUFFED GRAPE LEAVES WITH EGG-LEMON SAUCE
(dolmadakia me avgolemono) | 7

An old-fashioned *mezze* (small dish; usually paired with alcoholic drinks), these meatballs are well balanced and unpretentious, with a touch of fresh spearmint and a hint of garlic. Best served with tzatziki sauce, salad, and pita bread. And, of course, a chilled glass of beer.

MEATBALLS
(keftedes)

Prep: 30 min | Cook: 25 min | Ready in: 55 min | Serves: 10–12

For the meatballs:
(3 pounds) 1.35 kilograms ground meat (combo beef, veal, and pork)
3 eggs
1 bulb garlic bulb, freshly minced
¼ cup freshly chopped spearmint
¼ cup breadcrumbs
½ tablespoon salt
1 teaspoon pepper

For frying:
flour
vegetable oil

DIRECTIONS

1. Combine the meat, eggs, garlic, spearmint, breadcrumbs, salt, and pepper into a bowl, and mix by hand.

2. Roll out into 1½-inch balls. Grease your hands with vegetable oil while rolling out the keftedes so they don't get sticky. Spread flour on a plate, and roll the meatballs in the flour to coat.

3. Preheat vegetable oil in a large skillet over medium-high. Pan-fry a batch of 10 to 15 meatballs at a time, for about 7 to 8 minutes, or until nicely browned outside and no longer pink inside. Drain them on a paper towel–lined plate. Repeat with the remaining meatballs.

4. Cool for a few minutes before serving with a dip.

ALTERNATIVE COOKING METHOD
Bake the keftedes in the oven at 350°F (175°C) for 25 minutes, or until browned.

This tasty vegetarian starter is traditionally made with fresh zucchini, though my mom uses pumpkin in its place. Alternatives like squash or other gourds and even cucumber can be used. *Kolokythokeftedes* are best served in the summertime during an early evening happy hour with a glass of Ouzo on ice. I'm already daydreaming of relaxing at a taverna on the Greek coast, sampling some pumpkin fritters and seafood mezze. Oh, the good life!

PUMPKIN FRITTERS
(kolokythokeftedes)

Prep: 20 min | Cook: 10 min | Ready in: 30 min | Serves: 4

4 cups freshly shredded pumpkin (use a cheese grater)
3 garlic cloves
¼ cup ground dry spearmint
½ teaspoon salt
½ teaspoon pepper
⅓ cup flour
vegetable oil (for frying)

DIRECTIONS

1. Thoroughly squeeze out all the water from the shredded pumpkin. Mince the garlic into tiny bits.

2. Combine all the ingredients into a bowl and mix by hand. Shape into 3-inch patties.

3. Preheat a frying pan with vegetable oil, medium-high. Fry for 3 to 5 minutes on each side, or until the patties are golden brown, yet still moist inside.

4. Drain the patties on paper towels. Serve hot with tzatziki, yogurt, or sour cream on the side.

"Goo-goo ga-ga." That is the sound most of my non-Greek friends make when they try my mom's *dolma* with egg-lemon sauce. Guess it brings them back to their infancy stage. . . . Not sure if it's the combination of the frothy egg and lemon sauce that sets them off, or the simplicity of ground meat and rice mixed together into a ball, then wrapped warmly and snugly in a leaf? Whatever the case, to all my non-Greek friends who have implored me for years to snatch this recipe from my mother: Here it is in all its glory!

STUFFED GRAPE LEAVES
WITH EGG-LEMON SAUCE
(dolmadakia me avgolemono)

Prep: 40 min | Cook: 1 h 15 min | Ready in: 1 h 55 min | Serves: 10-12

For the stuffed meat:

1⅓ cup uncooked Italian-style rice

2¾ pounds (1.25 kilograms) ground meat (combo beef, veal, and pork)

1 small white onion

2 eggs

¼ cup olive oil

¼ cup vegetable oil

1 tablespoon salt

1 teaspoon pepper

⅓ cup ground dry spearmint

50 large grape leaves

For the egg-lemon sauce:

3 eggs

¾ cup freshly squeezed lemon juice

DIRECTIONS

1. Wash the rice with cold water through a strainer. Chop the onion into tiny bits.

2. In a large mixing bowl, combine the ground meat, rice, chopped onion, eggs, olive and vegetable oils, salt, pepper, and spearmint. Mix all the ingredients by hand.

3. Roll a 2-inch ball of meat/rice mix. Lay a grape leaf flat on the palm of your hand, bumpy veins side facing up (not the smoother side facing up). Place the meatball on the base of the leaf. Turn the right and left blades of the grape leaf over the meatball, forming a straight, ruler-like shape. Then, roll the covered meatball to the tip of the leaf, forming a snug, tight roll. Repeat.

4. Add all the dolmadakia rolls into a large stockpot, creating 2 to 3 levels of rolls. Fill the pot with just enough water to cover the rolls, and bring to a hard boil. Next, reduce to medium heat, partially covering the pot. Feed the dolmadakia with additional hot water from a boiling kettle, if required. Cook for 50 minutes. Remove from heat and set aside.

5. With a ladle, extract 1½ cups of soup-type mixture from the pot. Beat the eggs in a mixing bowl, then slowly pour in the lemon juice and soup-type mixture. Finally, pour the fluffy egg-lemon-soup blend over the dolmadakia.

6. Cover the pot fully, let stand for 10 minutes before serving.

My mother's family home in the town of Nea Chora ("New Town") in Arcadia, Greece. No one has lived there in over forty years, wild shrubs have taken over, but it's still standing!

SOUPS & SALADS

Growing up in a Greek household, *fakes* was the annoyingly classic (Greek) Mama-Always-Knows-Best meal. For the rest of you, it was the equivalent of being forced to eat broccoli. It's funny how one's taste buds change as you get older. Today, I knock back bowlfuls of fakes with a great big smile on my face. Packed with essential vitamins, proteins, fiber, and good carbs, this meal is the ultimate comfort food. I take back what I said earlier—Mama DOES always know best.

LENTILS
(fakes)

Prep: 5 min | Cook: 1 h 5 min | Ready in: 1 h 10 min | Serves: 8–10

4 cups Laird-type green lentils
1 medium white onion
1 bulb garlic, freshly minced
3 bay leaves
½ tablespoon cumin seeds
1 teaspoon salt
½ teaspoon pepper
1 cup tomato juice
⅓ cup olive oil
¼ cup white vinegar

DIRECTIONS

1. Wash the lentils in cold water through a colander, and add them into a medium stockpot with 10 cups of water. Bring the pot to a boil.

2. Chop the onion into ¼-inch bits. Add the chopped onion, minced garlic, bay leaves, cumin, salt, and pepper. Stir, then boil for an additional 10 minutes.

3. Reduce to medium heat, partially covering the pot. Cook for 30 minutes. Keep a boiling kettle of water on the side, in case the soup requires additional hot water.

4. Finally, add the tomato juice, olive oil, and white vinegar. Stir, and simmer for 15 minutes.

5. Let stand for 5 minutes before serving. Feel free to add additional olive oil, vinegar, salt, and pepper to taste.

This classic soup is perfect for a cold winter's day. Made with meatballs and rice and polished with a creamy sauce, *giouvarlakia* are hearty, mouthwatering, and utterly addictive. Simplicity at its finest, the secret ingredient being the *avgolemono* (egg-lemon) sauce. Careful not to overthicken the pottage as it may get too lumpy (a very common mistake). Best served with bread to soak up all that yummy egg-lemon sauce.

EGG-LEMON MEATBALL SOUP
(giouvarlakia me avgolemono)

Prep: 30 min | Cook: 1 h 30 min | Ready in: 2 h | Serves: 8

For the meatballs:
1 medium onion
1 cup uncooked Italian-style rice
3.3 pounds (1.5 kilograms) ground meat (combo beef, veal, and pork)
2 eggs
2 tablespoons olive oil
1 tablespoon vegetable oil
¼ cup ground dry spearmint
2 tablespoons salt
1 teaspoon pepper

For the soup:
1 cup uncooked Italian-style rice

For the egg-lemon sauce:
3 eggs
¾ cup freshly squeezed lemon juice

DIRECTIONS

1. Grate the onion in a large mixing bowl with a cheese grater. Wash 1 cup Italian rice through a colander, and add into the bowl. Combine the ground meat, eggs, olive and vegetable oils, spearmint, salt, and pepper. Mix by hand and roll into 2-inch balls.

2. Half-fill a large stockpot with water and bring it to a boil. Drop the meatballs into the pot, partially covering with a lid. Boil for 10 minutes. Reduce to medium heat and cook for another 30 minutes. If required, feed the stockpot with additional hot water from a boiling kettle. Wash an additional 1 cup of rice and add into the pot, continuing to boil for an additional 30 minutes.

3. In a medium mixing bowl, beat the eggs with a hand mixer for 1 to 2 minutes, then drizzle in the lemon juice. With a ladle, slowly pour 5 ladlefuls of meatball broth into the bowl while continuing to blend until the mixture fluffs up. Finally, pour this mixture into the pot, and with a large spoon, carefully intermix the fluffy egg-lemon mixture with the meatballs and broth.

4. Partially cover the pot with a lid and let set for 10 minutes. Serve, salt and pepper to taste.

"Beans, beans, are good for your heart. The more you eat, the more you . . .!" Well, we all know the rest of this silly rhyme. . . . And every time Mama served us bean soup, my siblings and I broke out into song at the dinner table, foolishly thinking our folks couldn't understand a word in English. A swift slap against the back of the head kept us honest—at least until the next time this dish was served. Even today, we still sing this childish song whenever *fasolada* is served, murmuring the tune under our breaths, winking at each other while cautiously wary of those breakneck-speed backhanders. There's no denying it: my siblings and I are loutishly asinine. And this *fasolada* recipe is sinfully delicious. Caution: Just don't sing at the dinner table.

WHITE BEAN SOUP
(fasolada)

Prep: 10 min | Cook: 2 h | Ready in: 2 h 10 min | Serves: 6

18 ounces (500 grams) dry white beans (medium size)
1 tablespoon baking soda
3 medium carrots
4 medium celery sticks
2 medium onions
½ cup olive oil
¼ cup vegetable oil
1 tablespoon salt
1 teaspoon pepper
1½ cups tomato juice

DIRECTIONS

1. In a colander, wash the dry white beans, then add into a large stockpot. Pour in warm water, covering the beans by about 2 to 3 inches. Stir in the baking soda, and soak overnight; this causes the beans to expand and soften.

2. Chop the carrots, celery, and onions into ½-inch bits.

3. Bring the beans (only) to a hard boil. Partially cover the pot, lowering the heat to medium-high, then boil for an additional 20 minutes (or until the beans begin to split open).

4. Now, toss in the carrots, celery, and onions and stir. Increase the heat, bringing the pot back to a boil. Once the soup reaches the boiling point, lower the heat back to medium-high. Pour in the olive and vegetable oils, and toss in the salt and pepper. Stir, then partially cover the pot. Be mindful to feed the soup with additional hot water from a boiling kettle, if required. Stir occasionally.

5. Cook for 45 minutes, then pour in the tomato juice and mix. Continue to simmer for additional 30 minutes.

6. Remove from heat and let stand 5 minutes before serving. Salt and pepper to taste.

Another hearty soup ideal for those cold winter days. My family's recipe calls for chicken broth only, and not actual chunks of chicken. But no need to panic: after the broth has been cooked, the whole chicken is then baked in the oven and served as a main course alongside the *kotosoupa avgolemono* as the starter. Trust me: After you try this combination, you will always devour broth-starter protein and its resulting soup this way.

EGG-LEMON CHICKEN SOUP
(kotosoupa avgolemono)

Prep: 5 min | Cook and bake: 1 h 35 min | Ready in: 1 h 40 min | Serves: 6–8

For the soup:

4 pounds (1.82 kilograms)
    whole chicken
1 small onion (top layer
    peeled)
1 celery stick
1 carrot stick
3 cups kritharaki (orzo pasta)
oregano
paprika
salt
pepper

For the egg-lemon sauce:

4 eggs
¾ cup freshly squeezed lemon
    juice

DIRECTIONS

1. In a large stockpot, add the whole chicken and peeled onion and fill with water. Crack the celery and carrot sticks into pieces, and sprinkle salt into the pot. Bring it to a hard boil (about 10 minutes). Reduce to medium-high heat, and cook for an additional 40 minutes, partially covering the pot. Intermittently remove excess fat and scum by skimming the top with a slotted ladle or a small mesh sifter. This entire process will "cleanse" the whole chicken.

2. Remove the chicken from the pot and set aside on a baking dish to cool. Dispose of the onion, celery, and carrot, and pour the chicken broth through a strainer and into another large stockpot. Add 3 cups of fresh water into the broth and bring again to a boil. Now, toss in the kritharaki and boil for 15 minutes, stirring occasionally. Toss in 1 tablespoon of salt, and continue boiling for another 15 minutes. Remove from heat and set aside to cool for 10 minutes.

3. In the meantime, with a knife, cut the chicken open down the middle; don't split it entirely in half. Speckle the chicken with oregano, paprika, salt, and pepper. Preheat the oven to 395°F (200 °C) on the convection setting. (See Conversion Charts at back of

(Continued on page 18)

book if you have a conventional oven.) Pour 2 cups of water into the baking dish, and bake the chicken for 20 minutes, turning over midway.

4. In a medium-sized mixing bowl, beat the eggs with a hand mixer for a couple of minutes. Drizzle in the lemon juice. Then, with a ladle, slowly pour in 3 ladlefuls of chicken broth while continuing to blend until the mixture fluffs up. Add the mixture into the pot and, with a large spoon, carefully combine the fluffy egg-lemon mixture with the chicken broth. Partially cover the pot with a lid and let set for 10 minutes. Add salt and pepper to taste.

5. Serve the kotosoupa as an appetizer with the chicken as the main course.

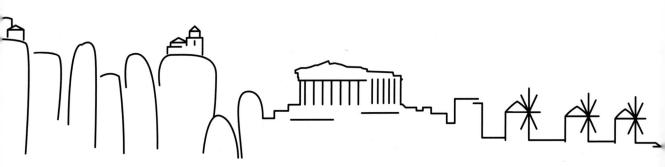

Also known as Easter Sunday Soup or Easter Lamb Soup, *magiritsa* contains the entrails and internal organs of the "sacrificial lamb," as well as greens and flavored seasonings. It's the prefect meal to break the Greek Orthodox fast (Lent). Dense and filling, the soup is traditionally prepared on Holy Saturday evening and eaten right after Easter midnight church service. Yes, I know, the insides of an animal sound kinda gross. But if you choose to be a carnivore, you must also respect the whole animal in its entirety, and not just the bits you like. Remember, the lamb has been given up for you, so the least you can do is try this recipe. Besides, it would be a total shame to waste these precious parts. (Yes, I am parroting my Baba word-for-word right now.) *Christos Anesti!* (Christ is Risen!) is the customary salutation when you greet someone after Easter midnight mass.

GREEK EASTER SOUP
(magiritsa)

Prep: 30 min | Cook: 1 h 30 min | Ready in: 2 h | Serves: 6

For the meat:

16 ounces (454 grams) lamb offal
  (internal organs and entrails)
1 small white onion
10 scallion shoots
5 leaves of andithia (curly endives)
5 leaves of romaine lettuce
vegetable oil
¾ tablespoon salt
½ teaspoon pepper
2 tablespoons olive oil
¾ cup uncooked Italian-style rice

For the egg-lemon sauce:

3 eggs
½ cup freshly squeezed lemon
  juice
chopped dill

DIRECTIONS

1. Clean and wash the offal thoroughly. Set aside.

2. Bring water in a large stockpot to a hard boil. Add the offal and blanch for 5 minutes; this will "clean" the organs. Drain the meat and cut up the offal into 1-inch cubes. Disregard excess fat and any undesirable bits.

3. Mince the white onion. Cut the scallions into ⅓-inch bits, the endives and romaine into 1-inch pieces.

4. Sauté the minced white onion with a splash of vegetable oil in a large saucepan over medium-high heat. Combine the organ cubes and sauté for a few more minutes. Pour in enough water to cover the meat, and partially cover the pan. Cook for 45 minutes, stirring occasionally. Feed the pan with boiling water from a kettle, if required. Add in the salt, pepper, and olive oil. Stir and cook for 15 minutes. Then combine the scallions, endives, romaine, and rice. Fully stir in the greens and cook the soup for another 15 minutes.

(Continued on page 20)

5. In a medium mixing bowl, beat the eggs with a blender for 1 to 2 minutes, then trickle in the lemon juice. Slowly pour 3 ladle spoonfuls of the soup into the bowl, continuing to blend until the mixture fluffs up. Add the mixture into the pot, and with a ladle, carefully intermix the egg-lemon sauce with the soup. Partially cover the pot, take it off the heat, and allow to rest for 10 minutes.

6. Top with chopped dill, and salt and pepper to taste.

The psilokomeni is by far my favorite Greek salad. It's naturally spicy *and* tangy but surprisingly refreshing and delicious. It's usually served during the winter months when other vegetables, like tomatoes and cucumbers, are out of season. Trust me, after you try this salad, you'll want to rediscover all varieties of plain greens again. There is beauty in simplicity.

PSILOKOMENI SALAD
(psilokomeni salata)

Prep: 5 min | Serves: 8

1 head romaine lettuce
3 scallion shoots
1 handful dill
olive oil
red wine vinegar
salt

DIRECTIONS

1. Wash and rinse the romaine lettuce, scallions, and dill in a colander. Allow the greens to dry.

2. Cut up the romaine and scallions into ⅓-inch pieces, and chop the dill finely. Toss all into a bowl.

3. Add olive oil, red wine vinegar, and salt to taste. Mix, then serve.

VARIATION
Squeeze lemon into the dressing, chop a small amount of red onion, and/or sprinkle tiny pieces of feta cheese (or any hard cheese) as a garnish.

The most overrated of all Greek salads. Don't get me wrong, I love *horiatiki salata*: it's so refreshing on a hot summer's day, it's actually thirst-quenching. But I've never understood the appeal to eat it throughout the entire year, rather than eating whatever vegetables are actually in season. So I strongly suggest serving up village salads when tomatoes have fully ripened, namely the months of July, August, and September. Buy tomatoes only if they're deep red, soft, and juicy. Think about it: the tomato is a fruit. It should always explode in your mouth with sweet delight, and summertime is always the best season for tomatoes.

VILLAGE SALAD
(horiatiki salata)

Prep: 5 min | Serves: 4

4 small tomatoes
½ large cucumber
½ red onion
olives
3.5 ounces (100 grams) feta cheese
olive oil
oregano
salt

DIRECTIONS

1. Wash the tomatoes, cucumber, and onion, chop, then toss into a salad bowl. Toss in the olives (as many as you'd like) and crumble in the feta cheese.

2. Add olive oil, oregano, and salt to taste. Mix, then serve.

EXTRA
Add watermelon squares, or other seasonal fruits like berries. Better yet, toss in orange slices!

Church of the Virgin Mary ("Panagia") bell tower in Nea Chora, Arcadia, Greece.

VEGETABLES

Fasolakia heal whatever ails you. I love trimming green beans tips with my fingers. (Please don't use a knife.) Feeling, stroking, touching—transferring your energy into your food—works; trust me. It's like when you water your flowers, plants, vegetable gardens, and herbs: you should always touch and talk to them. Because, just like children, we hope they will grow up to be wonderful and beautiful. And remember—*fasolakia* are made to be slurped back, so don't feel embarrassed to do so. Just make sure to submerge your bread into the juicy broth for an extra kick. And feel free to crumble some feta on top for added taste.

GREEN BEANS
(fasolakia)

Prep: 10 min | Cook: 1 h | Ready in: 1 h 10 min | Serves: 4

6 large handfuls green beans
2 celery tops and leaves (top half of celery stalks only)
1 medium onion
½ cup olive oil
1 tablespoon ground dry spearmint
¼ cup vegetable oil
1 tablespoon salt
pepper
1 cup tomato juice

DIRECTIONS

1. Wash all the vegetables. Trim the green bean tips. Chop the celery and onion into ½-inch cubes.

2. Sauté the onion with the olive and vegetable oils in a large stockpot for 3 to 5 minutes on high heat. Toss in the green beans, stir, then partially cover the pot. Cook for 5 minutes, then reduce to medium-high heat.

3. Toss in the celery and spearmint. Stir, and partially cover the pot. Cook for 10 minutes.

4. Mix in 3 cups of hot water from a boiling kettle. Cook for 15 minutes, stirring occasionally, making sure not to splinter the green beans.

5. Sprinkle in the salt and a dash of pepper, and add some additional hot water, if needed. Stir, partially covering the pot. Cook for another 15 minutes.

6. Pour in the tomato juice, and stir the soft vegetables carefully. Cook for a final 15 minutes or until the water has evaporated and an orange, oily broth remains. Remove from heat, and allow to sit for 5 minutes before serving. Goes great with bread and feta cheese!

Known as the Greek ratatouille, briami makes the perfect side dish. It's hearty, flavorful, and also works well as a full vegetarian meal. Many Greeks eat this as a main course during high-holiday fasting (Lenten) weeks, as it's hearty and filling.

BRIAMI
(briami)

3 medium zucchinis
3 medium eggplants
3 medium potatoes
4 small white onions
6 garlic cloves
1 teaspoon salt
½ teaspoon pepper
2 bay leaves
⅓ cup olive oil
¾ cup tomato juice

DIRECTIONS

1. Preheat the oven to 385°F (195°C).

2. Wash the vegetables and peel the potatoes.

3. Chop the zucchinis, eggplants, potatoes, and onions into ½-inch wedges. While cutting the vegetables, toss them straightaway into a large mixing bowl filled with water for 5 to 10 minutes, so they don't discolor.

4. Place the chopped vegetables into a large baking dish. Cut the cloves of garlic in half and chuck them in. Mix the salt and pepper onto the vegetables by hand, and add in the bay leaves. Finally, sprinkle the olive oil all over the veggies. Pop the dish in the oven, and bake for 20 minutes, allowing the vegetables' natural liquids to ooze out.

5. Stir in 1 cup of hot water from a boiling kettle. Bake for an additional 20 minutes, then pour in the tomato juice. Mix the vegetables with a large spoon.

6. Lastly, bake for another 30 minutes or until the vegetables have been thoroughly roasted. Keep rousing the veggies occasionally, making sure they don't stick to the baking dish. Add additional water, if required. Remove from the stove and let cool before serving.

NOTE
Cooking time varies with different potato varieties.

Stuffed vegetables recipes are found in all parts of the world. Considered the symbol of summer because of its vibrant colors, the Greek variation of *gemista* ("stuffed with") calls mainly for tomatoes, bell peppers, zucchinis, and eggplants. Though it's known as a super healthy and juicy vegan dish, you can always add minced meat into the stuffing should you require a boost of protein. For extra taste, try crumbling feta cheese on top.

STUFFED VEGETABLES
(gemista)

Prep: 1 h 15 min | Bake: 1 h 45 min | Ready in: 3 h | Serves: 5–6

3 medium zucchinis
3 medium eggplants
3 medium green peppers
3 medium tomatoes
3 medium potatoes, divided
1 large white onion
1 bulb garlic
1 cup uncooked Italian-style rice
½ cup finely chopped fresh spearmint
½ cup olive oil
¼ cup vegetable oil
⅓ cup tomato juice
1 tablespoon salt
½ tablespoon pepper

DIRECTIONS

1. Wash the first four vegetables and carefully cut open the crowns (about ¼ from the top). Thoroughly scoop out the insides with a spoon, keeping the innards for the stuffing. NOTE: Disregard the green pepper guts, as they're mainly empty and filled with seeds.
2. Chop the vegetable innards into ½-inch bites, and toss into a large mixing bowl. Thinly chop 1 potato, onion, and garlic (the other 2 potatoes will be used later on), and add into the bowl. Combine the rice, spearmint, olive and vegetable oils, tomato juice, salt, and pepper. Mix all by hand.
3. Preheat the oven to 385°F (195°C).
4. Place the hollowed-out vegetables into a large baking dish and spoon in stuffing. Then, cover the vegetables with their pre-cut crowns (tops). Cut the 2 remaining potatoes into ¾-inch wedges, drizzle a touch of tomato juice, and sprinkle salt and pepper on top of them. Arrange the potato wedges in the baking dish. To finish, pour 1 cup water into the baking dish, and drizzle vegetable oil and tomato juice on the stuffed vegetables with a final dash of salt.
5. Bake for 1 hour and 45 minutes. Pour additional hot water into the baking dish from a boiling kettle, if required. Remove from the oven, and let stand for 20 minutes before serving.

ALTERNATIVE BAKING METHOD
For a protein version, add 225 grams (8 oz) of any preferred minced meat in step #2.

Horta vrasta is probably the healthiest staple in Greek households. Two little known facts: 1) The Greek word for vegetarian is *hortofagos*, which means "weed-eater"; and 2) most people mistake the word *horta* solely for dandelion greens. The word actually means "greens" in Greek. And in Greece, there are heaps of greens that fall into this category. For example, the island of Crete claims over 100 edible wild mountain greens native only to that island. So, for this recipe, use any greens you like. My mom usually cooks with two varieties—chicory and curly endives—as they're more abundant in North America. She sometimes even adds boiled potatoes into the mix. Healthy *and* heavenly.

BOILED DANDELION GREENS
(horta vrasta)

Prep: 10 min | Cook: 15 min | Ready in: 25 min | Serves: 4–6

1 large head radikia (chicory)
1 large head andithia (curly endives)
olive oil
juice from 1 fresh-squeezed lemon
salt

DIRECTIONS

1. Wash and trim the stems of the radikia and andithia greens. Bring a large stockpot to a hard boil.

2. Separately boil the radikia and andithia greens, stirring continually. Cooking time is approximately 10 minutes for the radikia and 5 minutes for the andithia—or until both are slightly tender when poked with a fork.

3. Cool the greens by rinsing with cold water through a colander.

4. Combine both greens into a bowl. Top with olive oil, lemon juice, and salt to taste.

A simple vegetarian dish, *bamies laderes* are an acquired taste. I wasn't a great fan of this meal as a child, but I've come to love it over time. Stewed okra combines the best of both savory and sweet tastes and is served as a side together with a meat dish or as a light meal.

STEWED OKRA
(bamies laderes)

Prep: 15 min | Cook: 45 min | Ready in: 1 h | Serves: 4

20 ounces (570 grams) okra
dash of vinegar (to "prep" the okra)
dash of salt (to "prep" the okra)
2 medium white onions
⅔ cup olive oil
¼ cup vegetable oil
1 tablespoon salt
1 teaspoon pepper
1 cup tomato juice

DIRECTIONS

1. Trim both ends of the okra, then wash through a colander. Place the okra in a mixing bowl, sprinkle vinegar and salt, and mix by hand; this will allow the okra's inner moisture to ooze out via the tiny holes from the trimmed bottom ends. Let stand for 10 minutes, then rinse the okra again with water.
2. Cut the onions height-wise and toss them in a medium stockpot. Pour in the olive and vegetable oils, and sauté the chopped onions over high heat for approximately 3 to 5 minutes, or until the onions yellow. Stir frequently.
3. Toss the okra into the pot, combine. Pour hot water from a boiling kettle to cover the vegetables. Bring the pot to a boil. Reduce to medium-high heat, partially covering the pot. Cook for 10 minutes.
4. Toss in the salt and pepper. Mix delicately, so the okra do not split open. Boil for another 10 minutes, while feeding the pot with additional hot water, if necessary.
5. Pour in the tomato juice, stirring very carefully. Alternatively, shake the pot so the ingredients combine without having to stir with a cooking spoon. Finally, cook for 15 minutes, then set aside, keeping the pot partially covered.
6. Cool for 5 minutes before serving. Sprinkle additional salt and pepper to taste. Serve with bread.

BONUS
Crumble feta cheese over the okra for extra flavor.

The exterior walls of the original old Church of the Virgin Mary.

SAVORY PIES

SPINACH PIE (spanakopita) | 40

PUMPKIN PIE (kolokythopita) | 43

CHEESE PIE TRIANGLES (tyropitakia) | 44

SPINACH PIE TRIANGLES (spanakopitakia) | 47

Hands down, there is no better vegetarian pie. (And I'm not biased because of my Greek heritage.) It's healthy, rich, and savory, and just one bite simply reminds me of home. You can also make it with puff (dough) pastry, and switch out (or use a lesser amount of) the spinach and replace it with dandelion greens, chard, and/or leeks.

SPINACH PIE
(spanakopita)

Prep: 30 min | Bake: 45 min | Ready in: 1 h 15 min | Serves: 10

For the filling:
10 ounces (284 grams) spinach
6 scallion shoots
2 cups freshly chopped dill
3 eggs
½ cup uncooked Italian-style rice
5.3 ounces (150 grams) feta cheese
3 tablespoons olive oil
2 tablespoons vegetable oil
½ tablespoon salt
½ teaspoon pepper

For the crust:
10 phyllo dough sheets
olive oil
vegetable oil

DIRECTIONS

1. Wash the spinach, scallions, and dill. Cut the spinach and scallions into ½-inch pieces. Trim the stems off the dill, and chop into tiny bits. Add the greens to a large mixing bowl, crack in the eggs, toss in the rice, and crumble in the feta. Combine the olive and vegetable oils, salt, and pepper, then mix all ingredients by hand.

2. Preheat the oven to 350°F (175°C).

3. Grease a round 12-inch baking dish with vegetable oil. Place 4 phyllo dough sheets into the dish, making sure the phyllo edges overlap the baking dish. Lightly drizzle olive and vegetable oils over the phyllo. Add the spinach mixture and spread evenly throughout. Fold back in the exposed edges of the phyllo dough sheets over the spinach mixture, and sprinkle both oils over the folded-back sheets. Then, cover 3 additional phyllo dough sheets over the spanakopita, wrapping around the pie like a snug, cozy blanket. Once again, lightly drizzle both olive and vegetable oils over the phyllo. Finally, add 3 more phyllo dough sheets over the pie and sprinkle oils over them. Gently pre-cut the spanakopita into 2-inch squares, being extra careful not to perforate all the way through to the bottom. Spray water droplets all over the pie; this will stop the phyllo dough sheets from drying and cracking while baking.

4. Bake the spanakopita for 45 minutes or until the phyllo dough delicately browns. Let stand for 30 minutes before serving.

Much like the *kolokythokeftedes* (pumpkin fritters) from the appetizers section, Mama chooses to bake *kolokythopita* with pumpkin and not zucchini, as is the norm for both recipes. My guess is she "Americanized" this meal to integrate into her new homeland, perhaps during Thanksgiving season. Whatever the case—be it family or non-Greek friends—whoever eats at her place gobbles up the *kolokythopita* like there's no tomorrow! The raisins are the pièce de résistance, adding a sweet, chewy aftertaste.

PUMPKIN PIE
(kolokythopita)

Prep: 1 h 20 min | Bake: 1 h | Ready in: 2 h 20 min | Serves: 10

For the pie crust:
½ pound (¼ kilogram) softened Crisco (all-vegetable shortening)
5 cups all-purpose flour
½ tablespoon salt
1½ cups warm water

For the filling:
13 cups freshly shredded pumpkin
1 cup freshly chopped onion (¼-inch bits)
1 cup raisins
1 cup uncooked Italian-style rice
¼ cup ground dry spearmint
¼ cup olive oil
¼ cup vegetable oil
1 tablespoon salt

DIRECTIONS

1. In a large mixing bowl, mix by hand the all-vegetable shortening, flour, salt, and warm water; start with 1½ cups water, adding additional increments of ¼ cup at a time, if required. Continue kneading the pie dough by hand (about 10 minutes). Then, cover the dough with wrap so it doesn't dry up. Allow it to stand for 30 minutes; this will allow it to slightly rise and thicken.

2. Combine all the filling ingredients into a mixing bowl. Mix by hand.

3. Preheat the oven to 375°F (190°C).

4. Flatten the dough with a rolling pin; use flour to avoid sticking. Shape out two (2) crusts: one to line the baking dish, and one for the top-crust. Grease a round 15-inch baking dish, and carefully position in the bottom crust. Drizzle some olive and vegetable oils onto the bottom crust, spreading out evenly. Add in the filling and lay out equally. Fold over the overlapping crust ends, then cover the pie with the top-crust. Lather a touch of both oils on top. Pre-cut the pie, taking care not to reach the bottom; this will allow the pie to breathe and bake evenly. Finally, drizzle water on top so the pie crust softens.

5. Bake for 1 hour, or until golden brown. Allow the pie to completely cool before serving.

Oh my, the ultimate finger food! As a savory dish, I like to lather up *tyropitakia* with tzatziki sauce and shove a half dozen into my mouth, usually without even taking a breath. Washing it down with a cold beer is usually what saves me from choking to death. And now for something sweet. . . . Try dipping hot *tyropitakia* in Greek honey and drizzle on sesame seeds or crushed nuts. Darn, I need more beer. . . .

CHEESE PIE TRIANGLES
(tyropitakia)

Prep: 40 min | Bake: 30 min | Ready in: 1 h 10 min | Serves: 8

For the filling:

2 eggs
¼ cup shredded Romano
    cheese
5.3 ounces (150 grams) feta
    cheese
7 ounces (200 grams) soft
    ricotta cheese
1 tablespoon milk
1 teaspoon pepper

For the phyllo pastry:

8 ounces (227 grams) phyllo
    dough sheets
melted butter

DIRECTIONS

1. In a mixing bowl, combine the eggs, the three cheeses, milk, and pepper. Use a potato masher to fully mix the ingredients. Pour in additional milk by the spoonful, if required to soften the filling.

2. Lay out the phyllo sheets onto a large cutting board and slice 3-inch-wide strips. Cover the strips with a tea towel so they don't dry up. Brush each strip with melted butter, piling 3 strips for use per individual cheese pie triangle. Plop a teaspoonful of cheese filling onto the bottom edge of the 3 strips and fold the phyllo over like folding a flag. Repeat with remaining filling and phyllo, and arrange the triangles onto a greased baking sheet. Lightly brush the triangles with the remaining butter.

3. Preheat the oven to 350°F (175°C) on the convection setting, and bake for 15 minutes on each side, or until golden brown. (See Conversion Charts at back of book if you have a conventional oven.)

4. Set aside to cool for 10 minutes. Serve with a dip.

Enjoy *spanakopitakia* (baby cousins of the spinach pie) on the go as a mid-morning or midday snack. Combine it with any Greek dip—*tzatziki, skordalia, tarama, tirokafteri* or *melitzanosalata*—for a colorful rainbow of delights.

SPINACH PIE TRIANGLES
(spanakopitakia)

Prep: 1 h | Bake: 30 min | Ready in: 1 h 30 min | Serves: 8

For the filling:

10 ounces (284 grams) spinach
10 scallion shoots
2 cups freshly chopped dill
1 cup freshly crumbled feta cheese
3 eggs
¼ cup olive oil
½ teaspoon salt
1 teaspoon pepper

For the phyllo pastry:

16 ounces (454 grams) phyllo dough sheets
olive oil

DIRECTIONS

1. Bring a large stockpot of water to a hard boil.

2. Wash the spinach, scallions, and dill. Do not cut the spinach. Chop the scallions into ⅓-inch bits. Rinse the feta through a strainer to wash off the brine and set aside.

3. Toss the scallions and dill into the boiling pot of water. Boil for 2 minutes before adding in the spinach. Stir and boil for another 2 minutes. Thoroughly strain the greens through a colander, and let stand before placing into a large mixing bowl. Crack in the eggs, and toss in the crumbled feta. Combine the olive oil, salt, and pepper, then mix.

4. Lay out the phyllo dough sheets onto a large cutting board and slice 3-inch-wide strips. Cover the strips with a towel so they don't dry up. Brush each strip with olive oil, piling 3 strips for use per triangle. Drop a tablespoonful of spinach filling onto the bottom edge of the strips and fold the phyllo over like folding a flag. Repeat with remaining spinach filling and phyllo, and arrange the triangles onto a well-buttered baking sheet. Brush the triangles with olive oil.

5. Preheat the oven to 350°F (175°C) on the convection setting. Bake the spanakopitakia for 15 minutes on each side, or until golden brown. (See Conversion Charts at back of book if you have a conventional oven.) Cool and serve with a dip.

Mountain view from my mother's home in Nea Chora, Arcadia, Greece.

DIPS & SIDES

Perhaps not the most popular of all Greek dips, *skordalia* (*skordo* means "garlic") packs a pungent punch. It's made with crushed garlic and a starchy base (usually potato mash). Nuts or moistened stale bread are used for the purée base on occasion, and it's typically served as a side with *bakaliaros* (see seafood chapter for recipes) and fried or roasted vegetables. Best of all, *skordalia* is extremely nourishing. It's a powerful antioxidant and anti-inflammatory, so it's great for your heart. And (it should go without saying), it's totally delicious.

GARLIC POTATO PURÉE
(skordalia)

Prep: 5 min | Cook: 25 min | Ready in: 30 min | Serves: 10–12

3 medium white potatoes
5 garlic cloves
1 cup olive oil
¼ cup white vinegar

DIRECTIONS

1. Peel the potatoes and boil for 25 minutes. Then, mash the potatoes with a hand masher in a mixing bowl.
2. Purée the garlic cloves in a blender; add a splash of olive oil to help liquefy the garlic.
3. Combine the mashed potatoes, puréed garlic, olive oil, and vinegar into a bowl, mix and serve.

BONUS
For added taste and presentation, garnish with olives and freshly chopped parsley.

Tzatziki is by far the most popular Greek dip. When people find out that I'm Greek, many respond by saying, "Oooh, I love tzatziki!" Which is like me saying to a white American: "I like ranch salad dressing." Seriously folks, enough. But everything has changed recently with the popularity of the Mediterranean diet. It's great to see the general population trying to "educate" themselves. So next time you meet an "ethnic," please spare us the nervous spasm. Just be cool and make eye contact; we won't bite. Tzatziki ("za-ZEE-kee"): hard to pronounce, more difficult to spell, easy to eat. Consume tzatziki with bread or slather onto your favorite grilled vegetables or meats. Just make sure to rinse with mouthwash before you kiss your loved one, because it's SOOOO garlicky.

TZATZIKI
(tzatziki)

Prep: 10 min | Serves: 6

2 cups Greek yogurt (ideally 10% or other high fat)
2 tablespoons minced garlic
1 tablespoon finely chopped fresh dill
¼ cup freshly grated cucumber
¼ cup olive oil
1 tablespoon vinegar
1 teaspoon salt
½ teaspoon pepper

DIRECTIONS

Combine all the ingredients into a bowl, mix, and serve. For additional taste, top with olives and drizzle olive oil.

So salty, but so tasty! *Taramasalata* is the most authentic of Greek dips. When we were young, my mom would make this on Clean Monday (Ash Monday, the first day of the Great Fast) because fish roe is technically not meat. It was accompanied by luscious, hot-out-of-the-oven *lagana* (unleavened flat bread). My siblings and I would scoop up heaps of tarama with the bread, leaving no scraps for our folks. We were a feisty bunch, knowingly aware there would be little or no fun food for at least another forty days. Today, my family serves this dip on a regular basis, so we've forgotten the thrill and excitement associated with it. . . . Shame. Nevertheless, *taramasalata* is my all-time-favorite mouthwatering Greek dip!

POTATO AND FISH ROE PURÉE
(taramasalata)

Prep: 5 min | Cook: 25 min | Ready in: 30 min | Serves: 10–12

3 medium white potatoes
½ cup carp caviar
½ cup olive oil
¼ cup freshly squeezed lemon juice

DIRECTIONS

1. Peel the potatoes and boil for 25 minutes. Mash the potatoes with a hand masher in a mixing bowl.

2. Combine with the remaining ingredients into a bowl and mix. Serve warm or chilled.

I'm not a big fan of fried foods, but this is fried perfection. And like potato chips, you can't just have one. I like dipping *kolokythakia tiganita* and *melitzanes tiganites* in tzatziki, or even adding them as leftovers in a sandwich the following day. Careful you don't bring your sandwich to work, otherwise you'll have to share!

BATTER-FRIED ZUCCHINI / EGGPLANT
(kolokythakia tiganita / melitzanes tiganites)

Prep: 10 min | Cook: 30 min | Ready in: 40 min | Serves: 6

3 small zucchinis
3 small eggplants
ground dry oregano
salt
pepper
flour
olive oil (for frying)

DIRECTIONS

1. Clean and cut the zucchinis and eggplants lengthwise into ¼-inch slices. Generously sprinkle oregano, salt, and pepper on the slices, then cover completely with flour on both sides.

2. Pour olive oil into a frying pan and set to high heat. Fry the zucchinis and eggplants separately, until golden brown, evenly cooking both sides.

3. Plop the fried zucchinis and eggplants onto a large plate covered with paper towels. Let cool for 5 minutes. Serve with a dip, or two!

Simply delicious and completely vegan, *gigantes* are made with large "giant" beans, first cooked then baked in an aromatic tomato sauce. Though considered a mezze, they're super-filling and divine. I can eat bowlfuls without the need of a main course. You can feel the sustenance radiating through your body just by looking at this beautifully colored dish.

BAKED BEANS
(gigantes plaki)

Prep: 30 min | Cook and bake: 45 min | Ready in: 1 h 15 min | Serves: 6–8

26½ ounces (750 grams)
   large lima beans
¼ cup olive oil
2 tablespoons vegetable oil
½ tablespoon salt
1 teaspoon pepper
1 cup tomato juice
2 tablespoons dry oregano
   (shredded)
freshly chopped parsley

DIRECTIONS

1. Wash the beans in a colander, place in a bowl, and soak in water overnight. Drain the water and peel the skins off the beans by hand.

2. In a large stockpot, cover the beans with water and bring to a hard boil. Reduce to medium-high heat. Add in the olive and vegetable oils, salt, and pepper, stir. Cook for 5 minutes, then set aside. Mix in the tomato juice.

3. Preheat the oven to 400°F (200°C).

4. Pour the beans into a 9 x 13-inch Pyrex baking dish, removing excess water/tomato juice, if required. Bake for 30 minutes, stirring occasionally.

5. Remove from the oven, mix in the oregano, and let set for 15 minutes to thicken before serving. Sprinkle additional salt and pepper to taste, and garnish with freshly chopped parsley.

My waistline keeps telling me I shouldn't be a big fan of carbs. My mom's *patates sto fourno* recipe calls for simple white potatoes—I know, very old school. But after you've tasted these, you'll want to experiment with the yellow, red, and even blue potatoes. Caution: There are more than four thousand varieties of potatoes, so your belly—like mine—may not be that forgiving.

OVEN-BAKED POTATOES
(patates sto fourno)

Prep: 15 min | Bake: 1 h 15 min | Ready in: 1 h 30 min | Serves: 6

12 medium white potatoes
1 large lemon
1 tablespoon dry oregano
   (shredded)
1 tablespoon salt
½ teaspoon pepper
½ teaspoon paprika
6–8 garlic cloves
olive oil
vegetable oil
4 tablespoons of butter
water

DIRECTIONS

1. Preheat the oven to 400°F (200°C).
2. Peel the potatoes and cut into wedges, tossing them directly into a bowl of water; this way the potato wedges don't discolor. Let stand for 5 minutes.
3. Drain the water from the bowl. Cut the lemon in half, squeezing the juice out with a fork over the potatoes. Sprinkle on the oregano, salt, pepper, and paprika.
4. Place the potatoes in a baking dish. Add in the garlic cloves, then drizzle olive and vegetable oils over the potato wedges. Drop the butter in four separate spots on the baking dish, and pour in 1 cup water. Bake for 60 minutes. Then, pour in ½ cup water, as some will have evaporated. Bake for another 20 minutes.
5. Remove from the oven, transfer into a serving dish. Let cool for 10 minutes before serving.

NOTE
Cooking time varies with other potato varieties.

Flags adorn the Church of the Virgin Mary on Assumption Day (August 15). The townspeople traditionally serve boiled goat ("gida vasti") and you can find the recipe in the cookbook.

PASTA & RICE

SPINACH WITH RICE (spanakorizo) | 65

HILOPITES (hilopites) | 67

SPAGHETTI WITH CHEESE (makaronia me tyri) | 68

An easy-to-make classic, *spanakorizo* is the Greek cousin to the mighty Italian risotto. It can also be used as a great base for a much heartier meal: simply mix in soft veggies, pre-cooked meat or seafood, and presto! You have a nourishing bowl of goodness that will warm your heart. In your face, Italian cousin!

SPINACH WITH RICE
(spanakorizo)

Prep: 5 min | Cook: 40 min | Ready in: 45 min | Serves: 4

7 ounces (200 grams)
   spinach
2 scallion shoots
4 cups water
½ cup uncooked Arborio rice
   (risotto rice)
½ tablespoon salt
2 tablespoons olive oil

DIRECTIONS

1. Cut the spinach into 1-inch bits, and finely chop the scallions.

2. In a saucepan, bring 4 cups water to a rapid boil. Add the rice, salt, and olive oil. Stir vigorously for about 3 to 5 minutes, then toss in the spinach and scallions. Stir for an additional minute.

3. Turn off the heat, but keep the pan on the stove element, and cover almost completely. Let set for 30 minutes, or until the rice thickens. Serve.

EXTRA
Squeeze some lemon on top, plop chunks of feta cheese on the side, and serve with bread.

Hilopites are small, square egg pasta, the name loosely breaking down as *hilos* (porridge) and *pites* (pies). On my first vacation to Greece as a young child, I remember visiting mountain village homes and staring at women, in awe, as they made this pasta, then cut them into a million pieces by hand. They would then spread them onto bed sheets to dry out. I'd wonder: Why would anyone go through all this trouble for a simple, teeny-tiny pasta? But then I tasted the freshly made hilopites, and I was immediately hooked! The lesson in all this: Goodness is found in the smallest forms. Used mainly as a side dish or a base for heartier meals that include beef and chicken, hilopites on their own are usually considered more of a soup than a pasta dish. Quick and easy to make, this go-to dish satisfies hungry bellies in a flash, especially kids. And if you can score some *mizithra* cheese (hard to find outside Greece, but worth the trouble!), this meal instantly goes to another level. Oh yeah, and feel free to slurp; it would be insulting to the hilopites gods if you didn't!

HILOPITES
(hilopites)

Prep: 5 min | Cook: 25 min | Ready in: 30 min | Serves: 4–6

2 cups hilopites pasta
2 tablespoons olive oil
⅓ cup tomato juice
salt
pepper
grated Romano cheese (or
    Parmesan)

DIRECTIONS

1. In a saucepan, bring water to a hard boil. Add the hilopites, then reduce to medium-high heat. Pour in the olive oil and tomato juice, and pitch in several dashes of salt. Cook for 15 minutes, stirring often. Remove from heat.

2. Sprinkle pepper and grated cheese, to taste. Serve.

Everyone has a "last meal" request. I think *makaronia me tryi* may just be mine. C'mon, seriously—you can't go wrong with spaghetti lathered with butter and topped with *mizithra* cheese (butter and cheese being my two favorite food groups). Another simple, easy, and delicious pasta dish, *makaronia me tryi* is heaven on Earth. So, when I pass on one hundred years from now, I will devour more than just a bowlful. And then there's my "last dessert" request . . . Jeepers! My afterlife will just have to wait, I guess. Forget it, I'm never gonna die. In fact, none of you will if you make my mom's recipes. *Kali Orexi!* (Bon appétit!)

SPAGHETTI WITH CHEESE
(makaronia me tyri)

Prep: 5 min | Cook: 25 min | Ready in: 30 min | Serves: 4

16 ounces (454 grams) spaghetti (or long macaroni)
⅓ cup butter
mizithra cheese

DIRECTIONS

1. In a saucepan, bring water to a hard boil. Toss in the pasta, and cook for 8 minutes, stirring occasionally.

2. Remove from heat, cover the pan with a lid. Let stand for 10 minutes for pasta to thicken, then fully strain.

3. In a sauté pan, combine the pasta and butter over low-medium heat. Stir until spaghetti is well coated.

4. Sprinkle grated mizithra cheese on top. Serve immediately.

A centuries old abandoned home. Notice the doors (and windows) were smaller back then. This was due to a number of factors, such as keeping the cold weather out, and as a form of defense to keep enemies away. Also, floor-level heights in earlier centuries were different back then, and of course, shorter floors meant stronger building integrity, especially if the home was a multi-level stone house.

MEATS

Giouvetsi epitomizes the simplicity of Greek peasant cuisine. Made up of just a few ingredients with a slow cooking and baking time, it's hands down my favorite Greek meat dish. Nothing beats giouvetsi on a cold winter night. It's hearty, nourishing, soul-feeding, and I can't have just one serving. I LOVE coating it with a massive amount of shredded cheese, as if a snowy, wintry blast just hit a bowl of meat. Yum!

GIOUVETSI
(giouvetsi)

Prep: 10 min | Cook and bake: 2 h 20 min | Ready in: 2 h 30 min | Serves: 6

For the meat:

3.3 pounds (1.5 kilograms) front shank veal (or chicken or lamb)
salt (pinch)
white vinegar (sprinkle)
1 tablespoon olive oil
2 medium onions
2 tablespoons vegetable oil
½ cup tomato juice
½ tablespoon salt
¼ teaspoon pepper

For the pasta:

2 cups kritharaki (orzo pasta)—or hilopites or spaghetti
½ cup tomato juice
Romano cheese

DIRECTIONS:

1. Cut the veal into 2-inch cubes; do not debone. In a large stockpot, pour in sufficient water to cover the meat. Toss in 2 to 3 dashes of salt, and drizzle in a touch of vinegar. Boil for 10 minutes. Skim the froth with a slotted spoon, then remove the meat and place into a bowl. Rinse the pot.

2. Pour the olive and vegetable oils into the stockpot. Chop the onions into ½-inch cubes, toss in, and sauté over medium-high heat. Add the veal cubes, and cover the meat with hot water from a boiling kettle. Partially cover the pot, and stir. Bring the pot to a boil, then reduce to medium-high heat. Feed the pot with boiling water, if needed. Continue cooking for 45 minutes, then mix in the tomato juice, salt, and pepper. Stir, partially cover the pot, and cook for another 10 minutes. Set aside.

3. Preheat the oven to 395°F (200°C).

4. Add the kritharaki to a large baking dish (ideally, a round clay baking dish), spreading the pasta around with your fingers. Mix in 4 cups of hot water from a boiling kettle, and bake. Stir occasionally, making sure the kritharaki doesn't stick to the dish, while allowing the pasta and water to reach a boil (about 15 minutes). Then, mix in the tomato juice, and combine the veal and its broth. Bake for 10 minutes. Turn off the heat, and let the giouvetsi stand in the oven for an additional 10 minutes, or until the pasta thickens.

5. Remove from oven. Let cool, then top with grated Romano cheese. Serve with bread and red wine.

When I get old and lose my teeth, I'll be comforted by the fact that I won't have to chew my *hirino fricassee*, as the pork in this meal just melts in your mouth. The sour and bitter taste of the lettuce and curly endive create a perfect yin and yang with the pork. There is no other dish with complementary flavors like pork fricassée. Oh yeah—the egg-lemon sauce rounds out this winning formula!

PORK FRICASSÉE
(hirino fricassee)

Prep: 15 min | Cook: 1 h 45 min | Ready in: 2 h | Serves: 6

For the meat:
3.3 pounds (1.5 kilograms)
   pork shoulder (boneless)
1 medium white onion
2 tablespoons vegetable oil
1 head romaine lettuce
6 scallion shoots
1 head curly endive (frisée)
3 tablespoons tomato juice
½ tablespoon salt

For the egg-lemon sauce:
3 eggs
¾ cup freshly squeezed lemon
   juice

VARIATION
Switch out the pork for lamb, beef, or poultry.

DIRECTIONS

1. Cut the pork into 1-inch by 6-inch chunks (do not remove the fat; this will allow the meat morsels to peel away from the fat while cooking). Chop the onion into ½-inch cubes.

2. In a large stockpot, with the vegetable oil, sauté the white onion for 2 to 3 minutes. Toss in the pork and add enough water to cover the meat. Partially cover the pot and bring to a boil, removing the foamy scum as the meat bubbles. Reduce to medium-high heat, and cook for 1 hour.

3. Wash the greens, chopping the scallions into 1-inch bits, and the romaine lettuce and curly endive into 3-inch pieces. In a medium saucepan, boil water, and slowly add in the greens to simply soften them; this takes only a few minutes. Remove from heat.

4. Add all the greens and tomato juice into the pork, and bring back to a boil (about 5 minutes). Add in the salt, then, reduce to medium heat and cook for 10 minutes. Remove from heat.

5. Separate the eggs whites from the yolks. In a mixing bowl, beat the egg whites with a hand blender. Slowly add the egg yolks, and continue mixing. Mix in the lemon juice. Next, remove 3 ladles of liquid only from the soup blend and pour into the egg-lemon sauce, while continuing to mix with the blender. Finally, pour the egg-lemon sauce into the stockpot. Shake the pot to help spread evenly everywhere. Cover the pot and let set for 10 minutes before serving.

Arni sto fourno is the typical Greek Easter meal—as everyone the world over knows! And when I was a kid, the Greek men—in the mainly immigrant neighborhood I grew up in—would pack up in ginormous 1970s-model American cars ("boats," we called them) and head out to the countryside on Holy Week, only to return hours later with live sheep stored in the trunks of the cars. This is not a joke. You see, rather than go to butchers, these old-school alpha-male types went straight to source—the farmer—to pick the perfect live alpha sheep themselves. Only the best for their families on Easter Sunday. Talk about farm-to-table! I guess it was also their way to connect with the "old country." Problem was, it wasn't the best thing for their own kids. Why? Because we would pet and fall in love with these lambs—even give them names—during those few hours in their temporary homes in the car garage. Then moments later . . . SLASH! I could go on with the rest of the story, but I don't want to gross you out. So enjoy your meal, please! I mean, we all know where animal protein comes from; there are no innocents here . . . just silent lambs. And scarred-for-life kids with huge mental healthcare bills.

ROAST LAMB
(arni sto fourno)

Prep: 5 min | Bake: 2 h 15 min | Ready in: 2 h 20 min | Serves: 12

15 pounds (7 kilograms) leg of
  lamb
salt
pepper
oregano

DIRECTIONS

1. Preheat the oven to 395°F (200°C).

2. Liberally coat the leg of lamb with salt, pepper, and oregano. Position the lamb on a grilling grate and into a stainless-steel baking dish. Place into the oven, and pour water into the pan. Bake for 90 minutes. Feed hot water from a boiling kettle into the baking dish, as required.

3. Now, turn the baking pan 180 degrees so the lamb bakes evenly. Then reduce to 375°F (190°C) and bake for an additional 45 minutes.

4. Remove from oven, and let cool before carving.

BONUS RECIPE
Do not pour out the roast lamb drippings from the bottom of the baking dish—see bonus recipe on page 79.

I guess forty days of fasting (Lent) during Easter time prepares Greeks for the ultimate, greatest feast of the year. So absolutely nothing goes to waste. Actually, this recipe is pragmatic: Use the entire sacrificial lamb out of respect for the animal, I say! It also helps that *makaronia me zoumi arniou* is deliciously juicy. I think the oregano gives it that ultra taste. Once you try it, you'll wish Greek Easter came 'round more than once a year.

SPAGHETTI
WITH ROAST LAMB DRIPPINGS
(makaronia me zoumi arniou)

Prep: 5 min | Cook: 15 min | Ready in: 20 min | Serves: 4

lamb drippings (see Roast
    Lamb recipe, p.77)
salt
pepper
oregano
9 ounces (250 grams)
    spaghetti
mizithra cheese

DIRECTIONS

1. Pour the roast lamb drippings into a saucepan. Try a spoonful; should it require additional salt, pepper, and/or oregano, sprinkle in and mix to taste. Pour in less than 1 cup full of water to slightly dilute the drippings, and bring to a rapid boil.

2. Add in the spaghetti, then lower the heat. Return to a boil, and cook for 10 minutes, stirring occasionally.

3. Remove from heat, but do not strain the spaghetti. Let the pasta stand so it thickens in the saucepan. Sprinkle on grated mizithra cheese. Serve.

ALTERNATIVE BAKING METHOD
Instead of boiling the pasta, bake in the oven at 350°F (175°C) for 30 minutes, stirring occasionally.

Hirino stifado is another flavorsome slow-cooking dish. Super hearty and filling, *stifados* (stews) are primarily meant for "tougher" cooking meats, which require longer cooking times. Not a big fan of pork? You can always substitute with red meat, poultry, or even game meat. Just don't try fish; they don't fare well, as fish should not be cooked for too long. Serve with fresh bread, as this stew is perfect for dipping.

PORK STEW
(hirino stifado)

Prep: 10 min | Cook: 2 h 20 min | Ready in: 2 h 30 min | Serves: 4

3.3 pounds (1.5 kilograms) pork
1 tablespoon salt (for blanching)
1 tablespoon white vinegar
1 bulb garlic
15 small white onions
3 tablespoons olive oil
2 tablespoons vegetable oil
1 tablespoon salt (for stewing)
½ tablespoon pepper
½ tablespoon cumin seeds
3 bay leaves
2 cups tomato juice
3 tablespoons red wine vinegar

DIRECTIONS

1. Chop the pork into 2-inch x 2-inch cubes, and place into a large stockpot. Pour water to cover the meat, stir in the salt and white vinegar, and bring to a boil. This process will blanch and "clean" the raw pork cubes.
2. Separate the cloves from the garlic bulb; peel the cloves. Peel the onions, and chop one onion only; do not chop the others. However, do pierce each remaining onion in three different spots to allow the aroma to "breathe out" while cooking.
3. Skim the pork froth from the boiling pot with a slotted spoon. Remove the pork cubes and place in a bowl. Dump the boiling water into the sink, and rinse out the pot.
4. Add the one chopped onion and olive and vegetable oils to the pot, and sauté on medium-high heat. Then toss in the pork cubes. Reduce to medium heat, and brown the meat for about 5 minutes. Pour hot water from a boiling kettle to cover the pork. Add salt, pepper, cumin seeds, and bay leaves, and stir. Partially cover the pot, and increase to high heat. Once the pot reaches a hard boil, reduce to medium-high and cook for 20 minutes. Toss in three garlic cloves only, and continue cooking for an additional 20 minutes.
5. Add the whole onions and remaining garlic gloves to the pot and stir. Partially cover the pot, and bring back to a hard boil. Feed with hot water from a boiling kettle, if needed, but do not cover over the pork and onions. Lower the heat to medium-high and cook for 20 minutes. Stir in the tomato juice and red wine vinegar, and continue cooking for 20 minutes. Set aside, and let cool before serving.

Normally served during colder months (hunting season), *kouneli stifado* is a classic stew. Packed with nutrients, the rabbit is perfectly balanced with sweetly stewed white onions, spicy garlic, and fragrant seasonings. My family's recipe is killer... bunny killer, that is. 'Til this day, when my siblings and I find out my folks are cooking rabbit stew, we make sure to find an excuse to invite ourselves over for dinner. "Mama, Baba, do you need anything fixed around the house?" Or, "The grandkids really miss you guys . . ." Yeah, right!

RABBIT STEW
(kouneli stifado)

Prep: 10 min | Cook: 1 h 45 min | Ready in: 1 h 55 min | Serves: 6

3.1 pounds (1.4 kilograms) medium rabbit
1 medium white onion (chopped)
1 bulb garlic
25 small white onions
white vinegar
1 teaspoon cumin seeds
3 bay leaves
½ cup olive oil
1 teaspoon salt
¼ teaspoon pepper
½ cup red wine vinegar
1½ cups tomato juice

DIRECTIONS

1. Chop the rabbit into 3-inch pieces. Chop the medium onion into ¼-inch bits. Separate the cloves from the garlic bulb; peel the cloves. Peel the 25 small onions, slice off the tops and bottoms, and carve thin cuts (or small jabs) into each onion. This will allow the whole onion's flavor to seep out. In a saucepan, bring the small onions to a fast boil for about 2 to 3 minutes, then remove from heat.

2. Bring a large stockpot to a fast boil, squirt in some white vinegar, then add in the rabbit. Boil for 2 to 3 minutes. This removes the foamy "scum" from the meat. Strain the rabbit, and rinse out the pot. Place the rabbit back in the pot, fill enough water to cover the meat, and bring back to a boil (about 10 minutes).

3. Toss in the medium (chopped) onion, garlic cloves, cumin, and bay leaves. Partially cover the pot, and cook on high heat for 15 minutes. Pour in the olive oil, and with the pot partially covered, cook for another 15 minutes, stirring occasionally. Reduce the heat to medium-high, and cook for an additional 10 minutes.

4. Combine the salt, pepper, and small onions into the stockpot. Continue cooking on medium heat for 10 minutes, pot partially covered. Stir in ½ cup of red wine vinegar. Cook for 10 minutes, then pour in the tomato juice. Finally, cook for 20 more minutes, or until the meat has slightly separated from the bones.

5. Remove from heat, and let cool before serving.

The tradition goes like this: When shepherds would shave their livestock once a year—usually done in June before the extreme summer heat of July and August—they would invite the whole village to assist them. Shearing, clipping, and trimming a few hundred sheep or goats in one day on your own was next to impossible. So, for the villagers' troubles, the shepherd would serve *vrasto* (boiled meat), offering up one of his animals for sacrifice, normally a goat. And of course, live music, additional mezze, and jugs of wine were par for the course. I remember attending my first such event as a child, marveling at the camaraderie, the song and dance. It felt like I was part of a joyous Roma circus! And that boiled goat . . . oh my. Tasty, peppery, succulent—it was unlike anything my adolescent North American self had come across. When I returned home after my vacation, I demanded my mom immediately add *gida vrasti* to her regular menu. As a matter of fact, my mom's village typically serves boiled goat after church service on the morning of the Assumption of the Virgin Mary (August 15). Which means I make sure to visit Greece every August! The aromas, the pulling of the meat off the bones, the lapping of bread into the naturally fatty and salted broth, then sucking it back. . . . It's just divine.

BOILED GOAT
(gida vrasti)

Prep: 5 min | Cook: 2 h 40 min | Ready in: 2 h 45 min | Serves: 8

7 pounds (3.2 kilograms) goat ribs
2 long dry oregano stems (deleafed)
1 tablespoon salt
lemon
pepper

BONUS
Dunk chunks of bread into the broth—so yummy!

DIRECTIONS

1. Place the goat ribs into a large stockpot and cover with water. Boil on high heat for 40 minutes; this will "cleanse" the meat. Remove the ribs from the pot, and drain the water.

2. Place the ribs back into the pot, and once again cover with water, bringing to a hard boil. Throughout the cooking process, occasionally skim the meat scum from the surface. At the 1-hour mark, add two long deleafed oregano stems. Continue to boil for 10 minutes, then lower the heat to medium-high, and add 1 tablespoon salt. Boil for 50 additional minutes.

3. Remove the ribs from the pot, position into individual plates, and pour ladles of broth over the ribs. Squeeze lemon, and add pepper to taste. Serve.

No, it's not a spelling mistake. This meal is actually spelled *patsa*, and not *pasta*. In fact, this dish is a *pikti* (jellied) version of the original soup version of *patsa*. Normally cooked with tripe (animal stomach linings), my family's recipe calls for using an actual pig head and its feet. But for this specific recipe, we will use only a pig head. Yup, that's right. Not for the faint at heart . . . And if you're game, pig heads are not hard to come by. Most butchers will be relieved to sell you one, as they don't want to see them go to waste. Someone's scrap is another person's delight.

Pikti patsa is perfect for those cold, winter months: it's sharp and spicy and best served with lots of red wine. It also has a reputation for being a great hangover cure, as it apparently helps with digestion. Certainly not suitable for the thin-skinned, but you will be supremely rewarded, as *pikti patsa* is a great source of collagen—an ideal cure-all for your tendons and ligaments.

In some of my earliest memories, I recall my folks spending a full day cooking dozens of bowlfuls, our house smelling of spicy goodness. And, a day later, watching as our neighbors, friends, and family members showed up at our front doorstep with big smiles on their faces, knowing that they would be honored with a gift of jellied pig head and feet by the best *patsa* cooks around: my folks. Kinda reads like the opening pages of a Stephen King novel . . .

JELLIED TRIPE SOUP
(pikti patsa)

Prep: 1 h | Cook: 2 h 20 min | Ready in: 3 h 20 min | Makes: about 8 soup bowls

1 pig head
4 small freshly chopped chili
   peppers
½ cup garlic (minced)
⅔ cup freshly squeezed lemon
   juice
1 tablespoon salt

DIRECTIONS

1. Shave unwanted hair from the pig head with a razor. Place the head in a large stockpot and cover with water. Bring to hard boil, and continue boiling for 10 minutes; this process will "clean" the meat. Remove the head from the pot, and drain the water.

2. Place the pig head back into the cooking pot, and once again cover with fresh water, bringing to a hard boil. Continue to boil for 10 minutes, then reduce to medium-high heat and cook for 1 hour. Take out the pig head, but this time set aside the broth; it will be used later on. Allow the head to cool for about an hour.

(Continued on page 88)

3. "Pull" the meat from the pig head by hand. Discard the brain, eyes, tongue, and any small bones. Cut the remaining meat and fat into 1-inch cubes, then add the morsels back into the large cooking pot with its original broth. Reheat for 10 minutes on medium-high heat. Combine the chili peppers, garlic, lemon juice, and salt. Stir thoroughly.

4. Using a ladle, carefully pour the patsa into bowls. Set aside to cool for 3 to 5 hours at room temperature; the pork fat will congeal the broth into a gel. Place in the refrigerator overnight; allowing to fully solidify.

5. Always store in the refrigerator, but remove 10 minutes before serving.

VARIATION

Switch out the pig head for actual tripe (pig stomach lining) and eat immediately as a hot soup; do not congeal or refrigerate.

With its moderate climate and rich soil, Greece is blessed with every type of colorful flower you can imagine.

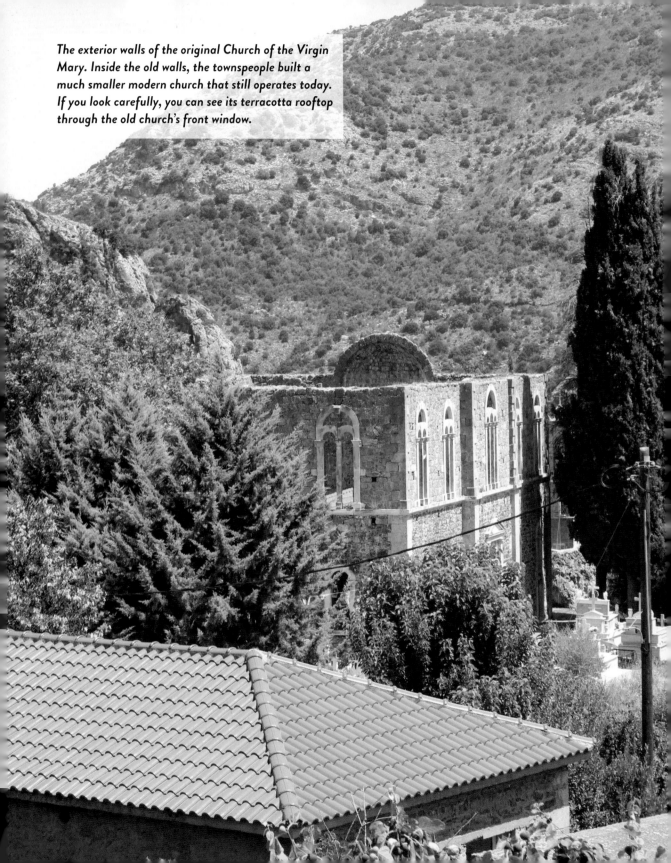

The exterior walls of the original Church of the Virgin Mary. Inside the old walls, the townspeople built a much smaller modern church that still operates today. If you look carefully, you can see its terracotta rooftop through the old church's front window.

MINCED MEATS

PASTICHIO (pastichio) | 93

MOUSSAKA (moussaka) | 95

KEBAB (kebab) | 99

Also know as the Greek lasagna, this pastichio recipe is very time-consuming. So pop open a bottle of red wine, put on an opera (preferably Maria Callas), and dig in. Trust me, it's worth it. The meat sauce is criminally good—that's why it takes 90 minutes to cook. Béchamel sauce is traditionally used in pastichio; however, my mother's recipe calls for a custard sauce made from scratch. In my humble opinion, it makes a world of difference. I'm salivating right now just writing about it.

PASTICHIO
(pastichio)

Prep: 15 min | Cook and bake: 2 h 15 min | Ready in: 2 h 30 min | Serves: 8

For the meat filling:
26½ ounces (750 grams) ground beef
26½ ounces (750 grams) ground veal
⅓ cup olive oil
⅓ cup vegetable oil
1 medium onion
½ tablespoon salt
½ teaspoon pepper
1 teaspoon sugar
3 cups tomato juice

For the pasta:
16 ounces (454 grams) long macaroni (bucatini)
4 eggs
½ cup butter
1 cup grated Romano cheese

For the custard sauce:
5 tablespoons custard powder
4 tablespoons flour
4 cups whole milk

DIRECTIONS

1. Add the beef and veal in a large stockpot and cover with water, mix. Bring to a boil. Once the meat browns, strain the meat with a mesh strainer (or fine colander) to remove the excess water. Rinse the pot.

2. Pour the olive and vegetable oils into the same pot, chop the onion into ½-inch cubes, and sauté. Add the meat, and once again pour water in (from a boiling kettle) to cover the meat. Toss in the salt, pepper, and sugar, and mix. Bring to a rapid boil. Then, lower the heat to medium-high to maintain a constant boil, partially covering the pot. Cook for 30 minutes, stirring occasionally. Add the tomato juice, and stir again. Lower the heat one notch and simmer 45 minutes, or until the water has essentially evaporated from the meat. Stir occasionally, so the meat doesn't stick to the pot.

3. In another large stockpot, bring water to a rapid boil. Add a few dashes of salt. Cook the long macaroni for 10 minutes (or al dente), stirring occasionally. Strain the pasta, and pop it back into the same pot. Add the eggs, butter, and grated Romano cheese into the pot and mix by hand.

4. Spread a ½-inch layer of meat sauce into 10 x 15–inch Pyrex baking dish. Add 1-inch layer of macaroni on top, then 1 inch of meat sauce.

(Continued on page 94)

Sprinkle additional grated Romano cheese. Finally, add one more layer of macaroni and meat sauce, sprinkling on some more grated cheese.

5. Preheat the oven to 350 °F (175 °C).

6. Whisk the custard powder, flour, and milk in a saucepan on low heat until the cream thickens. Then, liberally spread the custard cream evenly over the meat and macaroni. Sprinkle grated Romano cheese on top. Place in the oven and bake for 40 minutes, or until the custard cream sauce turns lightly golden brown.

7. Let set for 1 hour before serving; otherwise the pastichio is too "runny" to properly cut. Complement with a fresh side salad.

Moussaka is traditionally found in the Eastern Mediterranean and the Balkans, likely having Arab origins. The Greek version is made of three layers: potatoes and/or veggies on the bottom, red meat (preferably lamb) in the middle, and a cream sauce on top. My Mama's recipe includes potatoes, zucchinis, and eggplants as a base, a combination of three meats as the protein, and an egg custard sauce instead of béchamel. Possibly considered the "national dish" of Greece, moussaka is ideal for dinner parties. Pair it with a fresh salad or roasted red peppers with olive oil and a bottle of red wine.

MOUSSAKA
(moussaka)

Prep: 15 min | Cook and bake: 2 h 5 min | Ready in: 2 h 20 min | Serves: 8

For the meat filling:
14 ounces (400 grams)
    ground beef
11 ounces (300 grams)
    ground veal
11 ounces (300 grams)
    ground pork
1 medium onion
vegetable oil
1 teaspoon salt
¼ teaspoon pepper
2 cups tomato juice

For the vegetables:
3 medium potatoes
4 medium zucchinis
4 medium eggplants
1 teaspoon salt
vegetable oil (for frying)

For the custard sauce:
5 tablespoons custard powder
4 tablespoons flour
4 cups whole milk
grated Romano cheese

DIRECTIONS

1. Add the three ground meats to a large stockpot, pour water in to cover, then mix well. Bring to a boil. Once the meat browns, strain the meat with a mesh strainer to remove the excess water. Rinse the pot.

2. Chop the onion into ½-inch cubes, and sauté in the same cooking pot with vegetable oil (about 5 minutes). Add in the meat, and once again pour enough water (from a boiling kettle) to cover. Toss in the salt and pepper, mix, and bring to a rapid boil. Then, reduce the heat to medium-high, partially covering the pot. Cook for 30 minutes, stirring occasionally. Mix in the tomato juice and simmer for 45 minutes, or until the water has mostly evaporated. Stir occasionally.

3. While the meat is cooking, slice the potatoes in round shapes, much like chips—about ¼-inch thick. Same goes for the zucchinis and eggplants—¼-inch wide but cut length-wise. Toss the vegetables into a mixing bowl, sprinkle a ½ tablespoon of salt, and mix by hand. In a frying pan, fry the potatoes, zucchinis, and eggplants separately on medium-high heat—approximately 10 minutes per vegetable.

4. Preheat the oven to 350°F (175°C).

(Continued on page 96)

5. Now, in a saucepan, whisk the custard powder, flour, and milk on low heat until the cream thickens (about 8 to 10 minutes).

6. Finally, layer the potatoes on the bottom of a 9 x 13–inch Pyrex baking dish, followed by the zucchinis and eggplants. Spread the meat sauce all over. Cover with custard cream, and sprinkle grated Romano cheese on top. Place in the oven and bake for 40 minutes, or until the custard cream sauce turns lightly golden brown.

7. Let cool 1 hour before serving.

The signature dish of the Middle East and North Africa, kebabs probably made it up to Greece via the Ottomans. So delicious and packed with simple seasonings in each minty bite, kebabs are trouble-free to make. And you can't—nor would you want to—eat just one. So make sure to starve yourself hours in advance.

KEBAB
(kebab)

Prep: 30 min | Bake: 40 min | Ready in: 1 h 10 min | Serves: 6

2¾ pounds (1.25 kilograms) ground meat (mix of beef, veal, and pork)

2 eggs

½ teaspoon minced garlic

1 small onion, chopped

⅓ cup breadcrumbs

1 tablespoon salt

½ teaspoon pepper

¼ cup finely chopped fresh mint

¼ cup olive oil

DIRECTIONS

1. Combine the ground meat, eggs, garlic, onion, breadcrumbs, salt, pepper, mint, and olive oil into a large bowl. Mix by hand. Then, roll into 1½-inch x 6-inch cigar-like patties and pierce through with bamboo skewers; makes about 12 to 15 kebab brochettes.

2. Preheat the oven to broil.

3. Position the skewers onto a grilling grate and into a stainless-steel baking dish. Grill for 20 minutes on one side. Turn over the skewers, and grill for another 20 minutes.

4. Let cool before serving. Serve kebabs with pita bread, yogurt, salad, and potatoes or rice on the side.

An old wood-burning stove placed outside as a decorative ornament. These old stoves were used to heat up homes in the winter as well as cook and bake food.

POULTRY

Slow-cooked *kotopoulo me hilopites* in a basic tomato sauce is the most unpretentious and down-to-earth Greek meal you can eat. I morph into a kid when I think about it. And like a kid, you must eat the chicken with your fingers. Why? Because you're gonna want to suck back the tomato sauce and pasta found between the bones, tendons, and cartilage that's been simmering for hours—so good! If someone tells you it's impolite to eat with your fingers, they are not—I repeat, NOT—your friend. Dispose of them as fast as you toss out those chicken bones.

CHICKEN WITH HILOPITES

(kotopoulo me hilopites)

Prep: 5 min | Cook: 1 h 25 min | Ready in: 1 h 30 min | Serves: 6

2 medium onions
5 pounds (2.25 kilograms) chicken drumsticks (or other chicken sections)
salt (pinch)
1 tablespoon white vinegar
⅓ cup olive oil
¼ cup vegetable oil
2 tablespoons salt, divided
1 teaspoon pepper
2 cups tomato juice
18 ounces (500 grams) hilopites pasta
grated Romano cheese
pepper, to taste

VARIATION

Switch out the hilopites pasta for penne or long macaroni (bucatini). And, similar to a *pastitsada* recipe, use rooster instead of chicken—mmm, mmm . . . delicious!

DIRECTIONS

1. Clean and chop the onions into ½-inch squares.

2. Place the chicken drumsticks into a large stockpot, and pour enough water to cover. Stir in a dash of salt and 1 tablespoon of vinegar, and bring to a boil. Skim the chicken froth with a slotted spoon, then remove the chicken and place in a bowl. Rinse out the pot.

3. Pour the olive and vegetable oils into the pot, toss in the onions, and sauté over medium heat for a few minutes. Combine the chicken, 1 tablespoon salt, and 1 teaspoon pepper, and mix. Add enough hot water from a boiling kettle to cover the chicken, and increase to high heat. Cover the pot partially and bring to a boil (about 20 minutes). Then, lower the heat to medium-high and mix in the tomato juice. Continue to boil for 10 minutes, or until the chicken is properly cooked through. Remove the chicken with a slotted spoon, placing into a large bowl. Cover and set aside.

4. Mix the hilopites into the boiling pot of tomato broth. Feed additional hot water from a boiling kettle, if required. Stir often. Toss in 1 tablespoon of salt, and continue to stir. Boil over medium-high heat for 25 minutes, or until the pasta is cooked. Set aside.

5. Combine the chicken into the pot, cover, and let set for 15 minutes. Sprinkle grated cheese and pepper to taste.

Owing to the tarty lemon taste and slow roast time, *kotopoulo me patates sto fourno* melts in your mouth. Best of all, if you have a bread or pizza oven, try baking this on low heat for a few hours. It's worth the wait!

CHICKEN WITH OVEN-BAKED POTATOES
(kotopoulo me patates sto fourno)

Prep: 15 min | Bake: 1 h 15 min | Ready in: 1 h 30 min | Serves: 4

5 medium potatoes
1 lemon
oregano
salt
2 large whole chickens
pepper
paprika
olive oil
vegetable oil
2 tablespoons butter
7–8 garlic cloves

DIRECTIONS

1. Preheat the oven to 395°F (200°C).

2. Peel the potatoes and cut into wedges. Squeeze the lemon with a fork over the potatoes, then sprinkle oregano and salt. Arrange the potatoes wedges into a large stainless-steel baking dish.

3. Chop the chicken into desired portions, and place in a mixing bowl. Sprinkle salt, pepper, and paprika, and mix by hand.

4. Place the chicken pieces into the baking dish with the potatoes. Liberally drizzle olive and vegetable oils, and add in the butter. Pour ½ inch of water into the dish, and place in oven. Bake for 45 minutes, then remove from the oven. Now toss in the garlic; this way the cloves don't darken too quickly. Turn over the chicken and potatoes, then place the baking dish back in the oven.

5. Shift the chicken and potatoes occasionally so they don't stick to the pan, and feed the pan with hot water from a boiling kettle, if required. Bake for 30 minutes, or until the chicken is cooked through and the potatoes have softened.

6. Remove from oven, and let cool for 15 minutes before serving.

Perfect lounger on a hot summer day. "Lunch for two?"

FISH & SEAFOOD

OCTOPUS WITH PASTA (htapodi me kofto makaronaki) | 109

ROASTED COD WITH ONIONS AND POTATOES (bakaliaros plaki) | 110

PAN-FRIED COD WITH GARLIC AND POTATO PURÉE
(bakaliaros me skordalia) | 113

FRIED SARDINES (sardeles tiganites) | 115

Octopus is technically not considered a fish; it's a mollusk, much like a squid and even a clam. And scientists now consider it as intelligent as a primate, able to communicate not just among themselves, but with other fish. Fascinating. . . . Still, *htapodi me kofto makaronaki* is my all-time favorite Greek seafood dish. Served during Easter season (Great Fast), you can use just about any pasta for this recipe. My mother chooses "cut" macaroni as it clicks well with the small octopus morsels, almost surrounding the octopus—much like it does to its prey. Because it's a Lenten recipe, it's not topped with grated cheese, but please be my guest and smother it with the stuff. (I suggest grated *mizithra* cheese.) Shhh, I won't tell anyone you're breaking your fast. . . .

OCTOPUS WITH PASTA
(htapodi me kofto makaronaki)

Prep: 10 min | Cook: 1 h 10 min | Ready in: 1 h 20 min | Serves: 4

2.65 pounds (1.2 kilograms) octopus
salt (dashes)
white vinegar (sprinkles)
1 medium onion
½ cup olive oil
½ teaspoon pepper
⅓ cup white wine
1 tablespoon salt
1 teaspoon sugar
2½ cups "cut" macaroni
1 cup tomato juice

DIRECTIONS

1. Place the octopus into a stockpot and cover with water. Add 3 dashes of salt, and 3 sprinkles of vinegar. Bring to a hard boil. Once the octopus starts to boil (color changes from gray to red), remove from heat. Strain the octopus through a colander, and let stand for a few minutes. Cut the octopus into 1-inch morsels, and rinse with cold water.

2. Chop the onion into ⅓-inch cubes, and sauté in a cooking pot with ½ cup olive oil on high heat for a few minutes. Add the octopus, and continue sautéing for an additional 2 to 3 minutes; stir. Be careful not to allow the octopus and onion to stick to the pot. Mix in the pepper, then reduce to medium-high heat, stirring for about 5 minutes. Pour in hot water from a boiling kettle—enough to cover the octopus. Bring to a boil, and reduce to medium heat, partially covering the pot. Cook for 10 minutes, then mix in the white wine, salt, and sugar. Continue to cook for 1 hour, stirring occasionally and feeding the pot with boiling water from a kettle, if necessary.

3. Toss in the macaroni, combine, and bring to a boil. Reduce to medium heat, add in the tomato juice, stir. Partially cover the pot, stirring occasionally. Again, remember to feed the pot with additional boiling water, if required. Cook for 15 minutes.

4. Turn off the heat, but keep the pot on the stove element. Let set for 10 to 15 minutes to allow the octopus and pasta to thicken. Serve.

In the old days, fresh fish was a rare sight in Greek mountain villages. For centuries, villagers would walk hours, if not days, to the closest seaside town. Later, with the advent of the automobile, fishmongers and fishermen would drive through the hilltop towns at best once a week to flog the latest catch of the day. So in reality, dried cod was the only option for the omega 3-starved mountain Greeks. Baked right, *bakaliaros* is delightfully chewy, with the soft potatoes and sweet onions serving as the perfect companion.

ROASTED COD
WITH ONIONS AND POTATOES
(bakaliaros plaki)

Prep: 3 days + 10 min | Bake: 1 h | Ready in: 1 h 10 min | Serves: 4

12 small pieces bakaliaros
(dried and salted cod)
4 medium white potatoes
4 medium white onions
salt
pepper
1 cup olive oil
1 cup tomato juice
6 garlic cloves
3 bay leaves

DIRECTIONS

1. Desalinate the bakaliaros for 3 days in a container of water placed in the fridge. Change the water daily. This will also "thicken" the fish.

2. Preheat the oven to 395°F (200°C).

3. Wash and chop the potatoes and onions into ⅓-inch wedges. Toss them along with the fish into a large stainless-steel baking dish. Sprinkle salt and pepper to taste, and mix by hand. Pour in the olive oil and tomato juice. Toss in the whole cloves of garlic and bay leaves, and place in the oven. Make sure to shift the fish and vegetables occasionally so they don't stick to the pan. Bake for 1 hour.

VARIATION

Similar to a *psari plaki* (baked fish), switch out the cod for sea bass, snapper, halibut, or tilapia. And instead of tomato juice, use 2 large diced tomatoes.

A popular dish served year-round, largely because it's made with salted cod, which means you don't have to wait for cod fishing season to enjoy this dish. But *bakaliaros me skordalia* is traditionally associated with March 25. That's a double celebration for Greeks, being both Independence Day and *Evangelismos* (the Annunciation of the Virgin Mary). And speaking of doubling the fun, the cod is served with garlic and potato purée, the perfect match for these fried fish fritters (see Garlic Potato Purée recipe below). So while the fried fish will raise your blood pressure, the garlic will lower it on this fiery Greek Independence Day. *Zito i Ellada!* (Long live Greece!)

PAN-FRIED COD
WITH GARLIC AND POTATO PURÉE
(bakaliaros me skordalia)

Prep: 2 days + 10 min | Fry: 45 min | Ready in: 55 min | Serves: 4

For the pan-fried cod:

12 small pieces bakaliaros
    (dried and salted cod)
vegetable oil (for frying)
flour
salt
lemon wedges

For the garlic potato puree:

3 medium white potatoes
5 garlic cloves
1 cup + 1 splash olive oil,
    divided
¼ cup white vinegar

DIRECTIONS

1. Desalinate the bakaliaros for 2 days in a container of water, placed in the fridge. Change the water twice daily.

2. Preheat vegetable oil in a large skillet over medium-high. Flour the bakaliaros and pan-fry a batch of 6 at a time, for about 8-10 minutes, or until golden brown. Drain the fish on a paper towel-lined plate. Repeat with the remaining cod pieces.

3. Peel the potatoes and boil for 25 minutes. Then, mash the potatoes with a hand masher in a mixing bowl.

4. Purée the garlic cloves in a blender; add a splash of olive oil to help liquefy the garlic.

5. Combine the mashed potatoes, puréed garlic, 1 cup olive oil, and vinegar into a bowl; mix.

6. Sprinkle salt on top of the cod, and serve with lemon wedges and garlic potato purée.

Wherever I am in the world, eating *sardeles* takes me instantly to the Greek seaside. There's no better feeling on a blistering hot day than sitting at a taverna, table plopped right onto the sand, a slight breeze on your cheek, swigging back a cold beer, and stuffing yourself with the "health food store" of the sea. Filled with minerals and vitamins and rich in omega-3, I recommend consuming sardines on a regular basis. And because this oily fish is low in the food chain, it has very few toxins or contaminants. If you don't like sardines fried, simply plop them onto a barbeque and grill them for 3 to 5 minutes on each side until well charred. Make sure to baste them with *ladolemono* (olive oil and lemon), and sprinkle with dried oregano, salt, and pepper. I'm now melting under the scorching Greek sun. "Waiter, another cold beer, please!"

FRIED SARDINES
(sardeles tiganites)

Prep: 20 min | Fry: 15 min | Ready in: 35 min | Serves: 4–6

700 grams (1.5 pounds)
    sardines (about 40 small
    sardines)
vegetable oil (for frying)
½ teaspoon salt
½ teaspoon pepper
½ tablespoon dry oregano
flour
lemon

DIRECTIONS

1. With a fish fillet knife, cut open the sardines down the middle of the bellies, remove the insides, and rinse well under water through a colander. Set aside for a few minutes to remove excess moisture.

2. Preheat vegetable oil in a skillet over medium-high. Salt, pepper, and shred dry oregano over the fish. Then, flour the sardines and fry a batch of 20 fish at a time for about 3 to 5 minutes on each side, or until browned. Drain on a paper towel–lined plate. Repeat with the remaining sardines.

3. Squeeze lemon on top. Best served with boiled dandelion greens, bread, and white wine.

As you drive to my Mama's mountain village, there are beautiful wild flowers on the road as far as the eye can see!

DESSERTS

I remember devouring this cake when I was a kid, right before I became allergic to tree nuts as a teenager. Today, from the looks of guests who try Mama's *karidopita*, methinks she murders this cake! Best served with coffee or copious amounts of milk—especially if you serve yourself more than a slice.

WALNUT CAKE
(karidopita)

Prep: 15 min | Bake: 45 min | Ready in: 1 h | Serves: 6

For the cake batter:
1½ cups all-purpose flour
1 cup sugar
3 teaspoons baking powder
½ teaspoon baking soda
salt (dash)
4 eggs
250 grams unsalted butter, melted
1 teaspoon cinnamon powder
½ teaspoon clove powder
1 cup chopped walnuts

For the glaze topping:
1 cup water
½ cup sugar

DIRECTIONS

1. Preheat the oven to 350°F (175°C).

2. Combine the flour, sugar, baking powder, baking soda, and a dash of salt into a large bowl. Mix with a large fork.

3. In a separate bowl, whisk the eggs, melted butter, cinnamon, and clove powders. Combine these contents into the larger bowl, mix. Finally, mix in the chopped walnuts.

4. Pour the batter into a greased 8 x 8-inch Pyrex baking dish. Bake for 45 minutes. Poke a toothpick into the middle of cake; if it pulls out dry, the cake is ready.

5. For the glaze topping, add 1 cup water and ½ cup sugar in a small saucepan, and bring to boil. Remove from heat, and place the pan into a large bowl of cold water to cool off for 5 minutes, or until the boiling water vapors dissipate. Pour topping onto the cake and spread about with a spoon, covering all corners and edges. Let stand for 1 hour before serving.

My mother's *keik portokali* stands out in even my earliest memories. I fondly remember my folks buying a small crate of oranges every week and, each morning, manually hand-squeezing fresh juice for my siblings and me. The aroma of citrus in the air triggers some sort of deep-rooted, pleasurable dopamine in me. Come to think of it, us kids were so lucky and spoiled. Who hand-squeezes orange juice today, right?! Though, I like to think I love *keik portokali* not just for its orange and hint of cinnamon flavoring, but for its utter simplicity: it's such an easy cake to make. You just can't say no to orange cake!

ORANGE CAKE
(keik portokali)

Prep: 10 min | Bake: 35 min | Ready in: 45 min | Serves: 6

1 large orange
2½ cups all-purpose flour
1 cup sugar
2½ teaspoons baking powder
½ teaspoon baking soda
½ teaspoon vanilla powder
2 eggs
½ cup olive oil
½ cup milk
¼ teaspoon cinnamon powder

For the glaze topping:
Greek honey
sugar (sprinkles)

DIRECTIONS

1. Preheat the oven to 350°F (175°C).

2. Shred the orange rind into tiny bits. Squeeze the orange juice, making sure to strain out the seeds. Set aside.

3. Add the flour, sugar, baking powder, baking soda, and vanilla powder into a large bowl and mix with a large fork.

4. In a separate bowl, whisk the eggs, orange juice, orange rind, olive oil, milk, and cinnamon powder. Add the contents into the larger bowl and mix.

5. Pour the cake batter into a greased 8 x 8–inch Pyrex baking dish. Bake for 35 to 40 minutes. Poke a toothpick into the middle of cake; if it pulls out dry, the cake is ready.

6. Glaze the cake with honey, and sprinkle a light dusting of sugar on top.

VARIATION
Switch the orange for two lemons to make lemon cake, instead!

When European settlers arrived in the New World, they quickly learned how to cook and bake with ground corn, which was introduced to them by Native Americans. Soon, they created their very own recipes for using cornmeal in breads, which they, in turn, exported back to Europe. But unlike the Southern United States, where cornbread is considered a traditional staple at the dinner table, the Greeks enjoy *bobota* as a dessert and not as bread. Still, it's unassumingly delectable, and if you do decide to serve bobota as a side for your barbeque dishes or dunk it in chili con carne . . . I won't turn a blind eye. In fact, I'll probably join you!

CORNBREAD CAKE
(bobota)

Prep: 10 min | Bake: 35 min | Ready in: 45 min | Serves: 6

2 cups corn flour
½ cup all-purpose flour
1 cup sugar
2½ teaspoons baking powder
½ teaspoon baking soda
2 eggs
½ cup olive oil
¾ cup milk

DIRECTIONS

1. Preheat the oven to 350°F (175°C).

2. Add the corn flour, flour, sugar, baking powder, baking soda, eggs, olive oil, and milk into a bowl and mix.

3. Pour the batter into a greased 8 x 8–inch Pyrex baking dish. Bake the cake for 35 to 40 minutes until it browns. Alternatively, bake in a muffin pan for 15 minutes.

Although *pita* means "pie," my mother's *milopita* recipe is more like a cake and is usually enjoyed as a Greek breakfast treat. Moist, delicate, and lightly spiced, this apple cake will dissolve in your mouth.

APPLE CAKE
(milopita)

Prep: 30 min | Bake: 1 h 15 min | Ready in: 1 h 45 min | Serves: 12

For the apples:
6 apples
sugar (sprinkle)
cinnamon powder (sprinkle)

For the cake batter:
4 eggs
1 cup milk
1 cup olive oil (or vegetable oil
    or combo)
1½ cups sugar
4 cups all-purpose flour
4 teaspoons baking powder
2 teaspoons vanilla powder
1 teaspoon cinnamon powder

For the glaze:
Greek honey
powdered sugar
    (confectioners' sugar)

DIRECTIONS

1. Peel and cut the apples. Sprinkle sugar and cinnamon on top, mix in a bowl, and set aside.

2. Preheat the oven to 350 °F (175 °C).

3. Whisk the eggs, milk and olive oil in a small mixing bowl. In a larger bowl, combine the sugar, flour, and baking, vanilla, and cinnamon powders. Pour the liquid contents into the big bowl, and mix thoroughly with a large fork. Finally, add in the apples, carefully mixing with a spoon.

4. Pour the cake batter into a greased Bundt pan. Bake for 1 hour and 15 minutes, or until it lightly browns. Poke a toothpick into the middle of cake; if it pulls out dry, the cake is ready.

5. Allow the cake to rest for 30 minutes before removing from the pan. Lightly glaze with honey, and dust liberally with powdered sugar. Cut and serve.

OPTIONAL FRUIT
Switch out the apples for pears. In Greece, when pears are in season, they're absolutely divine and make for a great alternative!

Diples is the Greek word for "fold." Originating from Peloponnese (where my family is from), the dough is easy to prepare but difficult to fry. Offered up during big events—weddings, baptisms, moving into a house, opening up a business, New Year's celebrations, etc.—it's common for Greek ladies to work together to make massive batches, numbering in the hundreds or thousands. The folklore says that diples for weddings brings ("folds") the newlyweds together, becoming "one," and the honey brings in a "sweet" New Year. I don't know how accurate this is. But I do know that you can't have just one. Diples are so addictive and, without fault, always crumble all over you, so you're forced to lick up your mess. Poor, poor you . . . Makes you wanna start a business, buy a house, get married, and get baptized every year!

Little-known fact: In Mani—a dry, arid, wild, and historically poor region in the southern Peloponnese—their version of this recipe calls for flour and water only.

DIPLES
(diples)

Prep: 1 h 35 min | Fry: 45 min | Ready in: 2 h 20 min | Makes: about 75 diples

For the dough:
4 cups all-purpose flour
2 teaspoons baking powder
5 eggs
1 cup Ouzo
vegetable oil (for frying)

For the syrup and garnish:
1 cup Greek honey
½ cup water
1 teaspoon freshly squeezed
   lemon juice
crushed walnuts
cinnamon powder

DIRECTIONS

1. In a bowl, mix the flour and baking powder with a large fork. With your fingers, form a small hole in the middle of the mix. Crack in the eggs, mixing by hand, and slowly pour in the Ouzo, while continuing to mix. Knead the dough until all the flour has been absorbed. Cover with a damp tea towel, and set aside for 1 hour, allowing the dough to set.

2. In a large frying pan, preheat vegetable oil on high heat, careful not to burn the oil.

3. Form a baseball-sized lump of dough with your hands, cover with a dash of flour, and feed through a pasta maker (rolling) machine; you will need someone to assist you with the flattening. Start at level 1 thickness, and continuously refeed the dough through the machine for up to 7 level thickness settings; so flatten 7 times in total. The

(Continued on page 128)

dough will stretch out about 6 feet long. Now cut and form into 5 x 5–inch squares, and cover with a tea towel so they don't dry up.

4. Lower the frying oil heat to medium heat, and drop only one dough square into the oil; do NOT fry more than a square at a time, as they fry up fast! With two large forks, tap the square to fully submerge it into the oil. "Fold" over 2 to 3 times to form a rolled carpet shape and until lightly golden—about 3 to 5 seconds per square. Remove the fried pastry from the oil, and place on a paper towel–lined baking sheet to eliminate excess oil. Repeat the frying process with the remaining dough squares.

5. In a saucepan, combine the honey, water, and lemon juice. Heat and stir for a few minutes. Drizzle the syrup mixture over the diples, and sprinkle with crushed walnuts and cinnamon. Store in an airtight container.

These deep-fried pastries have recently become the rage across North America. All my non-Greek friends now clamor for Mama's *loukoumades* recipe, being cute and careful trying to pronounce it properly, like they're kissing my behind ("*lou-kou-MAH-dez*"). The word is borrowed from the Turkish word *lokma*, meaning "morsel," originally termed in the ninth century. There are claims that a honey cake first appeared as a dessert in ancient Greece, while others suggest the origins date back from the Romaniotes—ethnic Greek Jews who have lived in Greece for thousands of years—who prepared them as Hanukkah treats. Honestly, we don't give a hoot who created them, nor who borrowed, copied, or stole from whom. *Loukoumades* are simply transcendent. Perhaps it really took three cultures to perfect these bite-sized puffs that are light and fluffy on the inside, and golden-fried and crispy on the outside. Makes for the ideal "cheat treat"!

GREEK DOUGHNUTS
(loukoumades)

Prep: 40 min | Fry: 35 min | Ready in: 1 h 15 min | Makes: about 35 doughnuts

For the active yeast:
1 packet (0.3 ounces
   [8 grams]) traditional active
   dry yeast
½ teaspoon sugar
1 cup warm water

For the dough:
3 cups all-purpose flour
½ teaspoon salt
½ teaspoon vanilla powder
½ teaspoon anise seeds (whole)
freshly squeezed juice from
   1 medium orange
1 cup warm water
vegetable oil (for frying)

For the syrup and garnish:
Greek honey
cinnamon powder

DIRECTIONS

1. Combine the yeast, sugar, and warm water in a mug. Set aside for 5 minutes.

2. In a mixing bowl, thoroughly whisk the flour, salt, vanilla powder, anise seeds, orange juice, active yeast, plus 1 (additional) cup warm water, making sure there are no lumps. Cover with a damp tea towel, and set aside. Allow the dough to expand in size (maximum 20 minutes).

3. Pour vegetable oil into a skillet, about 2 inches deep. Heat the oil to medium-high.

4. Grab dough with your hand and squeeze; a dough ball will form within the circle between your thumb and index finger. Scoop it out with a teaspoon, and carefully drop into the skillet, forming them into ball shapes—about 10 to 12 doughnuts at a time. With a slotted ladle, continuously turn over the dough balls until they're evenly

(Continued on page 131)

fried and fully golden—about 5 minutes per doughnut. Remove the loukoumades from the oil and place in a paper towel–lined bowl. Repeat with the remaining dough. TIP: Keep the dough-ball-scooping teaspoon lubricated by placing in a glass of water between scoops.

5. Liberally drizzle honey on the doughnuts, and sprinkle cinnamon powder. Devour all the loukoumades immediately, as they're best served fresh and hot!

BONUS

Try different toppings like crushed walnuts, hazelnuts, caramel, or maple syrups, powdered sugar, chocolate shavings, and/or sesame seeds.

Also known as Greek Easter butter cookies, koulourakia were my all-time favorite childhood biscuits. "Why?" you ask. Well, I would dunk them into tall glasses of cold milk just before bedtime, sometimes eating 20 at a time. I mean, what was I thinking?! I can't even imagine my poor digestive tract twisting and turning while I slept. It's very fitting, considering *kouloura* means "round twisted shape." Did I suffer from carb-induced childhood nightmares? You betcha. Do I still devour them as a late-night snack before suffering from wild insomnia? Hell yeah!

KOULOURAKIA
(koulourakia)

Prep: 1 h 20 min | Bake: 40 min | Ready in: 2 h | Makes about 90 small cookies

16 ounces (454 grams) softened unsalted butter
12 eggs
2 teaspoons vanilla powder
3 teaspoons baking powder
1 teaspoon baking soda
1 cup warm milk
2 cups sugar
12 cups all-purpose flour

DIRECTIONS

1. Beat the softened butter in a bowl with a hand mixer on medium speed for 10 minutes. Separate the egg yolks from the egg whites. Pour in the egg whites only, beat for 5 minutes. Then, mix in the egg yolks, vanilla powder, baking powder, and baking soda, and continue blending for another 5 minutes. Add in warm milk and sugar, and beat for an additional 5 minutes.

2. In a large mixing bowl, add about half the flour (6 cups), then pour in the liquid mixture from step 1. Mix all the ingredients by hand. Carefully add the additional flour (6 cups), 1 cup at a time; this will allow the cookie dough to be kneaded uniformly until it's thick and heavy, just like bread dough. Also, the dough may require 1 cup more or 1 cup less of flour; so trust your judgment as you manually mix by hand. This process takes about 30 minutes, so please be patient.

3. Preheat the oven to 350°F (175°C) on the convection setting. (See Conversion Charts at back of book if you have a conventional oven.)

4. Lay out the cookies with your fingers on a pastry board, hand-shaping them into braided circles, hairpin twists, figure-eights, Greek letters, etc. If the dough sticks to the pastry board while

(Continued on page 134)

rolling out, knead in a little extra flour. Finally, glaze the top of the cookies with a brushstroke of whisked egg yolk.

5. Place the cookies on greased baking trays. Depending on the size of the cookies, you will require 4 to 5 baking trays. Bake for 40 minutes, or until slightly browned.

6. Allow the koulourakia to cool before storing in airtight containers. Serve with coffee or tea. Better yet—dunk in a cup of cold milk!

VARIATION

For a high-holiday fasting recipe, switch out the butter, eggs, and milk for 1½ cups freshly squeezed orange juice, 2 cups vegetable oil, 1 cup olive oil, and ⅓ cup Metaxa brandy.

A derivative of *koulourakia* and a very popular snack during grape harvest season, the word *moustokouloura* is derived from *moustos* (young wine) and *kouloura* (rounded twists). These grape-must cookies are made with *petimezi*, which is grape syrup taken from the juice of freshly pressed grapes before it's made into wine. If you can't find it at a local Greek market or bakery, you can easily make a comparable version with 100% Concord grape juice. Just add some sugar, and boil at medium heat for about 1 hour, skimming the froth often, until the juice thickens. Chewy, pliable, and lightly spicy, I gotta say my mom's moustokouloura are a *MUST!*

GRAPE-MUST SYRUP COOKIES
(moustokouloura)

Prep: 1 hr | Bake: 40 min | Ready in: 1 h 40 min | Makes: about 40 cookies

5 cups all-purpose flour, divided
1 cup sugar
1 teaspoon baking soda
1 teaspoon baking powder
½ teaspoon vanilla powder
1 tablespoon cinnamon powder
½ teaspoon clove powder
1 cup olive oil
2 tablespoons Metaxa brandy
1½ cups petimezi (grape-must syrup)
1 cup warm water

DIRECTIONS

1. In a large mixing bowl, combine only 2 cups of flour, sugar, baking soda, baking powder, vanilla powder, cinnamon powder, and clove powder, and mix with a large fork. Pour in the olive oil, brandy, petimezi, and warm water. Mix all by hand.

2. Add the additional flour (3 cups), a cup at a time; this process allows the dough to be kneaded uniformly. As well, the dough may require a tad more flour, or a tad less. So trust your judgment as you mix by hand.

3. Preheat the oven to 350°F (175°C) on the convection setting. (See Conversion Charts at back of book if you have a conventional oven.)

4. With your fingers, roll out the dough into long cylinders on a pastry board. Then, shape them into multiple circles, twists, figure-eights, etc. If the dough sticks to the pastry board while rolling out, knead in additional flour.

(Continued on page 136)

5. Place the cookies on greased baking trays. Bake for 40 minutes, or until browned.

6. Let the moustokouloura cool before storing them in airtight containers. Serve with coffee or tea.

NOTE

If you can't find petimezi at a Greek supermarket or bakery, try the following:

- Use grapes, peel off the skins, liquefy them in a blender, then run it through a colander.
- OR: Add moustos (young wine) in a saucepan, and boil it slowly until half the quantity is dissolved.
- OR: Use grape juice. It may not have the taste of grape-must, but it's a simple and cheap alternative.

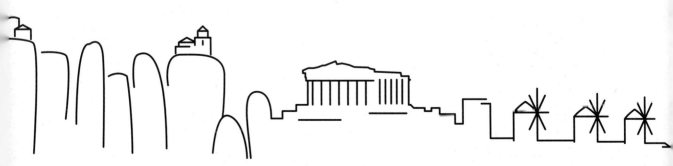

Here's to another Greek dessert made with *moustos* (young wine) and traditionally served during the autumn season! For this recipe, my mom does not use *petimezi* (grape-must syrup), but instead cooks with 100% Concord grape juice. Simple and easy to make, *moustalevria* is loved by all ages alike. Try making funny slurping noises, just like eating Jell-O. I know, it's a little juvenile to make sucking sounds at the dinner table, but hey, life's short!

GRAPE-MUST PUDDING
(moustalevria)

Prep: 5 min | Cook: 15 min | Ready in: 20 min | Makes: about 6 pudding bowls

For the pudding:
5 cups 100% Concord grape
   juice, divided
1 cup all-purpose flour
½ cup sugar
½ teaspoon cinnamon powder
⅛ teaspoon clove powder

For the topping:
cinnamon powder
walnuts (crushed)

DIRECTIONS

1. In a small mixing bowl, whisk 1 cup grape juice and 1 cup flour. Set aside.

2. In a saucepan, combine 4 cups grape juice, sugar, cinnamon powder, and clove powder. Mix and cook over medium heat for 5 minutes. Slowly pour in the grape juice/flour mixture from step 1, and continuously whisk over medium heat until the pudding thickens— about 10 minutes. If the pudding is too thick, dilute with a splash of water.

3. Remove from heat and immediately pour into pudding bowls. Sprinkle cinnamon powder and crushed walnuts on top. Let stand for a minimum 2 hours before serving.

BONUS
Top with other chopped nuts, sesame seeds, or diced fruits.

Rice pudding recipes are found in every corner of the world. The Greek version of *rizogalo* (which means "rice milk"; *rizi* and *gala*) is easy to make. Then again, stirring the rice mixture into a creamy and thick pudding is arduous and time-consuming . . . but entirely worth the trouble. My family's recipe calls for a tiny cinnamon stick bit to be tossed in during the stirring process, adding a hint of spice. Alternatively, you can add a strip of lemon rind (or orange) for a touch of citrus. Or just go all out and try both the cinnamon and citrus. Live on the edge, I say.

RICE PUDDING
(rizogalo)

Prep: 5 min | Cook: 1 h 20 min | Ready in: 1 h 25 min | Makes: about 6 pudding bowls

For the pudding:
1 cup long grain rice
1 cup water
6 cups whole milk
¼ cinnamon stick
1 cup sugar
1 egg (yolk only)
½ teaspoon vanilla powder

For the topping:
cinnamon powder

DIRECTIONS

1. Rinse the rice through a mesh strainer. Toss into a saucepan, mix in 1 cup water, and bring to a boil, stirring often on medium-high heat until the rice sucks up the water (about 10 minutes). Pour in the milk, and reduce to medium heat.

2. Toss in one quarter of a cinnamon stick. Cook for 30 minutes, whisking frequently so the milk doesn't curdle or stick. Then, add 1 cup of sugar, and continue cooking and stirring for an additional 40 minutes, or until the mixture has thickened. Remove the cinnamon stick bit.

3. Whisk the egg yolk and vanilla powder, then pour into the rice mixture. Mix well, and set the saucepan aside for 30 minutes for the rizogalo to cool, whisking occasionally; as it's cooling, the mixture continues to thicken. Pour into pudding bowls, sprinkle cinnamon powder on top, and refrigerate. Serve cold.

BONUS
Pitch in some raisins near the end of the cooking (step 3) for a bonus taste in every bite!

Greek yogurt is undoubtedly the most popular Greek export. Now that I mention it, there's also olive oil and feta cheese. And honey, wine, jams, saffron . . . Anyway, you know what I mean! And I know what you're thinking, *strangisto yiaourti* is technically not a dessert, right? Well, in Greece it is, as it's typically topped with honey, crushed walnuts, cereals, fruits, and the list goes on. In fact, beyond being a sinful snack, it's often served as a breakfast delight. That's good, as strained yogurt is highly nutritious, high in calcium, and a great source of protein with no cholesterol. Of all the recipes in this cookbook, this one is probably Mama's best-kept secret. So go nuts!

STRAINED YOGURT
(strangisto yiaourti)

Prep: 5 min | Cook: 1 h 15 min | Ready in: 15 h | Serves: 12

4 liters (1 gallon) 3.25% milk
6 ounces (175 grams) 6% Greek yogurt ("starter culture")
1 cheesecloth
2 small blankets

DIRECTIONS

1. Arrange a large glass bowl with a large metal stirring spoon inside; you will understand the reasoning behind this later.

2. Pour the milk into a large stockpot, and cook on high heat. Stir continuously to prevent the milk from burning and/or sticking to the bottom of the pot. Cook for about 30 minutes, or until the milk thickens and rises slowly to the top. Make sure the milk never actually boils. Remove from heat.

3. Pour the hot milk through a metal strainer and into the glass bowl. The large metal spoon inside the glass bowl acts as a heat absorber, conducting away the heat, which stops the glass bowl from cracking. Pour out ½ cup of hot milk and place on the side to cool; again, more information about this later. Stir the hot milk occasionally as it cools. Let the hot milk set for 45 minutes.

4. Mix the ½ cup cooled milk with the 6 grams (175 grams) 6% Greek yogurt ("starter culture"), and pour into the hot milk, stirring with a spoon. Cover the glass bowl with a glass top or plate. Carefully wrap 2 small blankets snugly around the glass bowl, and let stand for 10 hours. This cooling process will allow the milk to thicken and

(Continued on page 144)

the whey (remaining liquid) to separate from the milk.

5. Pour the unstrained yogurt from the glass bowl into the cheesecloth. Close the cheesecloth tightly, and hang over a basin to capture the excess whey. Allow it to strain at room temperature for several hours, or until desired thickness is achieved. Should you not have a proper place to hang the cheesecloth, try the method below (step 6). Otherwise, go directly to step 7.

6. Optional: (See note in 5). Rinse the glass bowl, and add the unstrained yogurt in its cheesecloth back into the bowl. Every 30 minutes or so, remove the excess whey from the glass bowl. Repeat numerous times, or until all the whey has been fully strained out.

7. Finally, remove the yogurt from the cheesecloth, using a large spoon and a dough spatula, if required. Place the yogurt in an airtight container, and refrigerate. It should keep well for about 1 to 2 weeks. When you're ready to make yogurt again, use 1 cup of the previous yogurt batch as the starter culture.

8. Top with Greek honey. Additional toppings may include crushed walnuts, fresh fruits and berries, cereals, granola, sour cherry syrup, jams, spoon sweets, etc.

Nothing screams Christmastime like melomakarona cookies. As a child, I remember the whole house smelling holiday-homey when Mama would bake these beauties. My siblings and I would mutter Robert Southey's nursery verse *"Honey (sugar) and spice and all things nice"* as we gorged ourselves on these cookies to the point of pain. In fact, these cookies have recently become so cool they're now made year-round, the best kind being chocolate-covered melomakarona. Insanely delicious, and totally hipster!

MELOMAKARONA
(melomakarona)

Prep: 1 h 10 min | Bake: 45 min | Ready in: 1 h 55 min | Makes: about 50 cookies

For the cookies:
1 cup olive oil
2 cups vegetable oil
1 cup freshly squeezed orange juice
3 tablespoons Metaxa brandy (or cognac or whisky)
1 cup sugar
1 teaspoon cinnamon powder
½ teaspoon clove powder
3 teaspoons baking powder
1 teaspoon baking soda
7 cups all-purpose flour, divided

For the syrup and garnish:
1 cup Greek honey
2 cups sugar
3 cups water
1 cup crushed walnuts
cinnamon powder (sprinkle)
clove powder (sprinkle)

DIRECTIONS

1. Combine the olive and vegetable oils in a bowl, and blend with hand mixer starting on low speed and slowly working up to medium speed. Then, slowly pour in the orange juice and brandy, and continue mixing. Add in the sugar, cinnamon powder, clove powder, baking powder, and baking soda. Mix for a total of 10 minutes.

2. In a large mixing bowl, start with 3 cups of flour, then pour in the liquid mixture from step 1. Mix all the ingredients by hand. Carefully add additional 4 cups of flour, 1 cup at a time; this will allow the cookie dough to be kneaded uniformly until it feels like bread dough. Also, the dough may require a touch more flour, so trust your judgment. The hand mixing takes about 10 minutes.

3. Preheat the oven to 350°F (175°C) on the convection setting. (See Conversion Charts at back of book if you have a conventional oven.)

4. Grease a couple of baking sheets with vegetable oil, or line with parchment paper. Roll out the melomakarona with your fingers, shaping them into 3-inch long by 1½-inch wide cookies and arrange them onto the greased baking trays. Bake for 45 minutes, or until lightly browned and baked through. Allow the melomakarona to cool

(Continued on page 146)

properly before proceeding to coat with honey and nuts.

5. Combine the honey, sugar, and water in a saucepan. Stir while bringing to a boil, then cook on low heat for 5 minutes. Skim the foam off the top. Now, here's where you need a helping hand: With a slotted spoon, fully immerse the melomakarona into the pan (about 5 to 6 cookies at a time) for about 2 minutes so the hot syrup thoroughly soaks through the cookies. Remove the melomakarona from the pan, place on a plate, and immediately garnish with crushed walnuts, then cinnamon powder and clove powder. Repeat with the remaining cookies.

6. Cool, then store in an airtight container. Serve with coffee or tea.

BONUS
Pour melted chocolate over the cookies immediately after you remove them from the saucepan (hot syrup), then garnish with walnuts, cinnamon powder, and clover powder.

The name *galaktoboureko* is a mouthful. It means "milk pie" (*galakto* and *borek*). This semolina-based custard pie covered in a crispy phyllo shell and soaked in sweet-lemon syrup is by far my favorite dessert. Galaktoboureko—a tongue twister name that will leave your taste buds wanting more!

GALAKTOBOUREKO
(galaktoboureko)

Prep: 55 min | Bake: 45 min | Ready in: 1 h 40 min | Serves: 16

For the syrup:
2 cups water
2 cups sugar
2 tablespoons freshly
    squeezed lemon juice
1 tablespoon lemon zest

For the pie:
6 eggs
6 cups milk
1 cup sugar
1 cup semolina
3 tablespoons corn starch
1 teaspoon salt
16 ounces (454 grams)
    softened butter
1 teaspoon vanilla powder

For the phyllo pastry:
12 phyllo dough sheets
melted butter

DIRECTIONS

1. In a saucepot, combine the water, sugar, lemon juice, and zest. Stir on high heat until the sugar is dissolved. At boiling point, reduce to medium heat, cook for 10 minutes. Remove from heat, and set syrup aside to cool.

2. In a mixing bowl, whisk the 6 eggs.

3. In a large stockpot, warm the milk on high heat, while carefully stirring for 5 minutes. Then, reduce to low-medium heat, and add in the sugar, semolina, corn starch, salt, and butter. Stirring, heat for 10 minutes. Then, slowly pour in the whisked eggs, and stir continuously until the custard mixture thickens—about 10 minutes. Remove from heat, then fully mix in the vanilla powder. Set custard cream aside.

4. Preheat the oven to 350°F (175°C).

5. Butter the bottom of a 9 x 13–inch Pyrex baking dish. Lay 6 phyllo dough sheets into the dish, brushing each sheet separately with butter. Pour in the custard cream, fold in the edges of the phyllo sheets, and cover with the 6 remaining phyllo sheets, brushing each with butter. Precut the pie before baking.

6. Bake for 45 minutes, or until golden brown. Shut off the heat, but keep the pie in the oven for an extra 10 minutes as the custard completes its simmer. Remove the pie from the oven, and liberally pour the syrup over top. Cool for a few hours before serving.

Originally brought to Greece by Greek and Armenian refugees from Asia Minor, the name *bougatsa* has Byzantine roots and is a derivative of the Italian word *focaccia* and the Turkish word *pogaca*, both being a type of bread. It's a custard filling breakfast pastry wrapped in multiple layers of phyllo dough and served hot out of the oven, but not before it's heavily dusted with powdered sugar. Every summer when I vacation in Greece, I go in search of the best local bougatsa before I hit the beach. That and a good slice of spanakopita usually sustain me up until my standard late-afternoon lunch. As for my mother, she typically serves it as dessert, baking a massive bougatsa a couple of times per year, making sure to invite the extended family over for dinner. And without fail, we sit back, gobsmacked, as we watch my older brother gobble up 4 to 5 servings in an instant!

BOUGATSA
(bougatsa)

Prep: 30 min | Cook and bake: 50 min | Ready in: 1 h 20 min | Serves: 12–15

For the pie:
9 ounces (250 grams) butter
6 cups milk
1 teaspoon freshly squeezed
    lemon juice
5 eggs
1½ cup sugar
1½ cup semolina

For the phyllo pastry and topping:
butter (for coating)
12 phyllo dough sheets,
    divided
cinnamon powder
powdered sugar
    (confectioners' sugar)

DIRECTIONS

1. Melt the butter in a saucepan.

2. In a stockpot, pour in the milk and lemon juice, then whisk in the eggs. Add the sugar and semolina, then place on medium-high heat. Whisk continuously, slowly bringing to a boil, until the custard cream thickens—about 10 minutes. Set the cream aside.

3. Preheat the oven to 350°F (175°C).

4. Butter the bottom of a round 15-inch baking dish. Lay 6 phyllo dough sheets into the dish, brushing each sheet separately with butter. Pour in the custard cream, folding in the edges of the phyllo. Then, cover with the 6 remaining sheets, again brushing each with butter.

5. Bake for 40 minutes, or until golden brown. Test by inserting a knife or toothpick in the center; it should come out clean. If it doesn't, keep in the oven and test in increments of 5 baking minutes. NOTE: Should any air pockets appear during baking, poke them down with a knife.

6. Allow the pie to cool for 10 minutes before lightly sprinkling cinnamon powder on top. Dust thoroughly with powdered sugar.

Greek spoon sweets (*glyka tou koutaliou*) have become wildly popular outside Greece, as they're used as toppings on Greek yogurt, frozen yogurt, and ice cream. They're made mainly with fruits, but sometimes with soft tree nuts, and are served in a teaspoon on a small plate to guests as a gesture of hospitality, accompanied by coffee and a glass of cold water. I'm a fanatic when it comes to spoon sweets, my favorite being sour cherry, though my mom makes quince and grape only. Now, don't get me wrong, I won't say no to her *glyka tou koutaliou*, especially when my mom serves them up in her dainty crystal glass dishes.

In my humble opinion, the quince can be a useless fruit when raw. It's tart and dull when consumed fresh, but when made into a preserve, it transforms itself into a rock star. In fact, the quince is yellow when raw, but when boiled into a preserve, it turns a bright, blood orange. It's a little hard and crunchy when biting down, but worth the trouble transforming this lowly fruit from tart to bloody rock star hot! Try to not overconsume as it's sweet as candy.

QUINCE SPOON SWEET

(glyko kydoni)

Prep: 15 min | Cook: 1 h 35 min | Ready in: 1 h 50 min | Makes: about 1½ liters

4 cups chopped quince (about 3 medium quince)
2 cups sugar
6 cups water
1½ tablespoons vanilla powder
1 cinnamon stick
2 teaspoons freshly squeezed lemon juice

DIRECTIONS

1. Peel and chop the quince into ¾-inch bits. Do not wash under water; the quince will discolor.

2. In a saucepan, combine the quince with sugar, water, and vanilla powder. Crack the cinnamon stick in half, and toss into the pan. Bring to a boil, then reduce to medium heat and cook for 1 hour and 20 minutes, stirring occasionally. Do not cover the pan. Mix in the lemon juice and continue cooking for 15 minutes.

3. Remove from heat, let cool for a couple of hours before pouring into preserve jars. Refrigerate.

The clove gives this grape spoon sweet a bold, hot, and spicy kick. In addition, the cinnamon and sugar make *glyko stafyli* so sweet that your teeth literally hurt—in a pleasant, masochistic kind of way. Fragrant and rich, the world's earliest sweeteners were actually made with preserved grapes, like *petimezi*—as described in earlier recipes (*moustokouloura* and *moustalevria*). Take time to enjoy this sweet. Savor it.

GRAPE SPOON SWEET
(glyko stafyli)

Prep: 5 min | Cook: 1 h | Ready in: 1 h 5 min | Makes: about 1½ liters

5 cups red grapes
2½ cups sugar
2½ cups water
½ teaspoon cinnamon powder
½ teaspoon clove powder

DIRECTIONS

1. Clean and destem the grapes. In a saucepan, combine the grapes, sugar, water, cinnamon powder and clove powder. Bring to a boil. Then, lower the heat to medium. Cook for 1 hour, stirring occasionally.

2. Remove from heat, and cool for several hours before adding into preserve jars. Refrigerate.

Kourabiedes are crumbly, buttery sweet shortbread biscuits heavily topped with powdered sugar. Along with melomakarona, they are the most popular Greek Christmas treats. They're served on other occasions, too, like Easter, name days, and baptisms. Their origins are seemingly from Iran (Persia), which is possibly the reason why they're formed into crescent shapes, along with the familiar round and egg shapes. Traditionally made with crushed almonds, my mom bakes kourabiedes without them due to my tree nut allergy, and I believe her recipe is all the better for it. As kids, we called them "cocaine cookies" because we would inhale these biscuits (and for their obvious appearance). Shows you where our minds were . . .

KOURABIEDES
(kourabiedes)

Prep: 1 h 20 min | Bake: 40 min | Ready in: 2 h | Makes: about 60 cookies

For the cookies:

32 ounces (908 grams) softened unsalted butter

2 eggs (yolks only)

¼ cup freshly squeezed lemon juice

½ cup Ouzo

2 teaspoons baking powder

2 teaspoons baking soda

2 teaspoons vanilla powder

4 tablespoons powdered sugar (confectioners' sugar)

8 cups all-purpose flour

For the topping:

powdered sugar (confectioners' sugar)

DIRECTIONS

1. In a large mixing bowl, beat the butter with a hand mixer for about 10 to 15 minutes until it's light and fluffy. TIP: Do not toss out any butter wrappers; you can use them later to grease the baking sheets. Combine the egg yolks, lemon juice, and Ouzo; beat for 1 minute. Finally, add in the baking powder, baking soda, vanilla powder, and powdered sugar. Blend the batter with the hand mixer for 5 minutes.

2. In another mixing bowl, add in the flour, then pour in the batter. Mix/knead manually by hand—about 20 minutes. Cover the biscuit dough with a moistened tea towel.

3. Preheat the oven to 350°F (175°C) on the convection setting. (See Conversion Charts at back of book if you have a conventional oven.)

4. Roll out the dough into round, long, or crescent shapes. Place onto greased baking trays, and bake for 35 to 45 minutes, or until lightly golden.

5. Remove the biscuits from the oven, place them on a sizeable, clean surface to cool for 1 hour. Sift powdered sugar over top until well-covered.

6. Store the kourabiedes in an airtight container. Serve with coffee or tea.

BONUS

For the traditional recipe, add a ½ cup crushed almonds or other nuts in step 2.

Greeks don't really go on about New Year's resolutions on January 1. Their biggest concern is the eternal question: "Who will get the good luck for the upcoming year?" And how that's decided is about as random as a coin toss. Greek families the world over look forward to slicing the *vasilopita* (king pie or Saint Basil's pie) after New Year's supper to reveal the lucky winner of the "lira coin." *Hronia Polla!* (Happy New Year!) And good luck to us all!

KING PIE
(vasilopita)

Prep: 10 min | Bake: 40 min | Ready in: 50 min | Serves: 12

For the pie:
4 cups all-purpose flour
1 cup sugar
2 tablespoons baking powder
1 teaspoon baking soda
1 teaspoon vanilla powder
1 teaspoon cinnamon powder
¼ teaspoon clove powder
zest from 1 medium orange
4 eggs
1¼ cup milk
1 cup freshly squeezed orange
    juice
1 cup melted butter
2 tablespoons Metaxa brandy
1 cup chopped dried figs
    (¼-inch pieces)
1 cup golden raisins
1 cup walnuts
1 coin (washed and wrapped in
    aluminum foil)
oil or butter (for greasing)

For the topping:
Greek honey
sugar (or powdered sugar)

DIRECTIONS

1. Preheat the oven to 350°F (175°C).

2. Shred the orange zest, and set aside. Then, squeeze the entire orange and set aside.

3. In a large mixing bowl, combine the flour, sugar, baking powder, baking soda, vanilla powder, cinnamon powder, clove powder, and orange zest. Mix with a large fork.

4. Whisk the eggs in a smaller bowl. Then add the milk, freshly squeezed orange juice, butter, and brandy. Whisk again.

5. Pour the liquid mix into the larger bowl. Add the figs, raisins, and walnuts. Mix thoroughly with a large fork (add additional milk, if needed). Toss in the vasilopita coin (a.k.a. "flouri"), making sure it's well hidden in the batter.

6. Grease a round 12-inch baking dish with oil or butter. Pour in the batter and place into the oven. Bake for 40 minutes, or until golden brown. Stick a toothpick or knife in the middle to check if it's fully baked. If not, bake for another 5 to 10 minutes.

7. Remove from the oven, and immediately glaze the top with honey, lathering freely with a pastry brush. Finally, lightly sprinkle sugar (or sift powdered sugar) on top of the honey glaze.

(Continued on page 160)

8. Let the pie cool overnight. Flip the top end over onto a large tea towel. Then flip topside up onto a cake plate or a pizza pan.

HOW TO SERVE

As for the pie-cutting ritual, there are numerous versions depending on local and family traditions. At my family's home, my father says a little prayer, does "the sign of the cross" over the pie with a knife, then cuts the first pie slice for the "house" to bless the home with good luck for the New Year. My dad then proceeds to slice additional pieces by order of age from eldest to youngest. The recipient who finds the hidden coin is considered "blessed" for the entire year. For the most part, with my family at least, I must say the winner has been pretty evenly distributed throughout the years. The message here: balance does exist in the world. So enjoy cutting this sweet, tasty cake. Just don't bite down too hard, or your first trip of the new year will be to the dentist chair.

The divine and majestic interior of the Church of the Virgin Mary in Nea Chora, Arcadia, Greece.

COFFEE & TEA

Also known as *sideritis*, which means someone "who has or is made of iron," Greek mountain tea is a natural antioxidant, rich in iron and known to fight off the common cold, flu, and other viruses. This herbal tea is wild, handpicked in high altitudes, growing on little or no soil at all, and oftentimes directly on the surface of rocks. Some of the best is found on the Parnon mountain range (1,935 meters or 6,348 feet high) just south of my Mama's village. On weekends, you usually see local farmers on the side of the road selling a bouquet for just a few euros. Priceless, I say, considering its boundless health benefits. I mean, just taking a deep whiff of dried *tsai tou vounou* feels like an instant cure-all. Beyond fighting off everyday viruses, it's been said that mountain tea strengthens the immune system, helps digestion, fights allergies, and is an excellent anti-inflammatory that reduces stress and even mild anxiety. With its rich aroma and unique taste, you need only sweeten it with honey. So please don't add sugar or you'll ruin the whole point of this handpicked, natural herb. The farmers in my mom's surrounding region will surely be displeased. Because at this price point, they're not climbing the mountains for their own benefit: they're doing it for you! Then again, I imagine when these farmers regularly hike up 1,000 meters and beyond, they do live longer, right?

MOUNTAIN TEA
(tsai tou vounou)

Ready in: 5 min | Serves: 2

2 tablespoons mountain tea (a.k.a. ironwort, a.k.a. "sideritis")
2 cups water
Greek honey

DIRECTIONS

1. In a briki pot, bring the tea to a hard boil, stirring occasionally. Once the water turns golden, remove from heat.

2. Strain the tea directly into a tea cup. Add Greek honey to taste.

Studies have shown that *ellinikos kafes* is good for your heart, contains high levels of antioxidants, and lowers your risk for diabetes. In fact, to this day, my folks drink a few cups per day—probably one of the many reasons they're still alive and kicking. And beyond what political party you support and at which beaches you vacation, the other most common fact Greek people need to know about you is "how you 'take' your coffee" *Sketos* (plain), *metrio* (1 part sugar), *glykos* (2 parts sugar), and even *varis* (2 to 3 parts coffee and 1 part sugar) are the different ways to prepare Greek coffee. Not much different than Turkish coffee (even though coffee is not actually grown in either country, so I never really understood this classification), this coffee is normally served with *paximathia* (biscotti), along with a glass of cold water. It's made with a fine grind, so it's meant to be sipped slowly as the grounds settle. Which means drinkers drift off, giving friends and family members time to shoot the sh*t. In fact, it's this relaxed pace of life that makes Greeks so . . . *Greek*. So, it's fitting that I end this book with this coffee. But be warned: This coffee is strong and heavy, and not for everyone. And don't forget to get your fortune read after you've finished it. Some people take this very seriously, and there are even books written about Greek and Turkish coffee readings. The most common readings are about . . . you guessed it: love, money, and health. So, here's to your well-being! And thank you again for reading this cookbook. *Yeia Mas!* (Cheers!)

GREEK COFFEE
(ellinikos kafes)

Ready in: 5 min | Serves: 1

1 tablespoon freshly ground Greek coffee

1 teaspoon sugar ("metrio")

water

DIRECTIONS

1. Preheat stove element to high heat.
2. Measure a full cup of water with a demitasse Greek coffee cup (or espresso cup). Combine with the coffee and sugar in a briki pot, stirring well, making sure to mix all three ingredients fully.
3. Heat the briki. As soon as the coffee boils up, quickly lift the briki pot from the hot element, and just as fast, tap the briki back onto the element for 1 second; the coffee will boil up again. Repeat one more time for a total of three quick "lifts" and two quick "taps." This will create the ideal amount of foam, also known as *kaimaki*. Note: This method varies depending on your specific stove element; gas, electric, etc. So please adjust accordingly, as you may only need 2 lifts and 1 tap. Pour the coffee carefully into the cup, taking care not to disturb the foam.
4. Serve with a glass of cold water and sweet cookies.

Juicy grapes hang liberally from vineyard arbors on village home verandas. Just watch your head as you get up to fetch an extra glass of wine!

Special Thank-Yous!

Beyond all my loving family members and friends that I have already credited on the copyright page, I would also like to thank the following people who supported me throughout this journey. Louise Fury, my relentless literary agent, who instantly fell in love with the concept of this cookbook and simply just gets me! Nicole Frail at Skyhorse Publishing for having faith in the project from the get-go, and understanding what it means to my Mama and her family. Teresa Lang, for coming up with the original title of the book, *Olive My Life*. Sorry, Teresa, I may just have to use it for my next book. :) My cousin Lambrini Sourligas, for helping my Mama out with the loukoumades, diples, and galaktoboureko recipes, as Mama's memory is fleeting at times—she knew the ingredients but simply forgot the directions for how to bake them. Tays Spencer of Appetite for Books, a cookbook bookstore in Montreal, for believing in me and pushing me to get this cookbook out to the rest of the world. Rick Thomas and Nancy Normand for having to put up with my madness while I was writing this book. Others include: Kathleen Hutchison, Ezra Soiferman, Max Cooke, Justin Kingsley, Leisa Lee, Jessica Reid, Sophia Hadzipetros, and dozens of friends and colleagues who have encouraged me throughout this process. And for those that I may have forgotten to mention, you are doubly thanked! And of course, my entire immediate family and relatives: I'm nothing without you. You all know that.

Greece is the third largest olive grower and a top consumer. Greeks use olive oil in their food, in their health and beauty products, and the list goes on. No wonder it's called the "tree of life"!

About the Authors

Christos Sourligas is an award-winning filmmaker, actor, writer, director, producer, storyteller. Christos has created and produced multiple feature films and television shows. As a former senior television executive for several internationally-renowned production companies, he's successfully brought shows into the homes of over 1.5 billion television viewers worldwide, airing in over 140 countries, and on 100 airlines. He also serves as a mentor and volunteer with various awards events, festivals, and non-profit organizations. Christos resides in Montreal, Canada, and travels often to his ancestral home in Arcadia, Greece, as well as other culinary destinations.

Evdokia Antginas was the proud mom of award-winning filmmaker Christos Sourligas. Evdokia was born in the mountainous region of Arcadia, Greece, known for its unspoiled wilderness and idyllic way of life. Surviving World War II and the devastating Greek Civil War, she always kept her head high while toiling away on factory farms. Having immigrated to Canada in the mid-1960s, she was married for over fifty years and had four incredible children and four equally awesome grandchildren. Evdokia felt best at home cooking up Greek and international delights for family and friends alike.

A majestic wild tree just outside my Mama's summer village near the Monastery of Panagia Malevi. This landscape glows magically when the sun sets!

Index

Lentils (fakes), 11
Octopus with Pasta (htapodi me kofto makaronaki), 109
Pan-Fried Cod with Garlic and Potato Purée (bakaliaros me skordalia), 113
Rabbit Stew (kouneli stifado), 83

W

Walnut Cake (karidopita), 119
walnuts
Diples, 127–128
Grape-Must Pudding (moustalevria), 139
King Pie, 159–160
Melomakarona, 145–146
Walnut Cake (karidopita), 119
White Bean Soup (fasolada), 14
wine

white
Octopus with Pasta (htapodi me kofto makaronaki), 109

Y

yogurt
Strained Yogurt (strangisto yiaourti), 143–144
Tzatziki, 53

Z

zucchini
Batter-Fried Zucchini / Eggplant (kolokythakia tiganita / melitzanes tiganites), 57
Briami, 31
Moussaka, 95–96
Stuffed Vegetables (gemista), 32

Nea Chora ("New Town") road sign just outside town. Every time I drive into my mother's village, I slow down . . . literally, and of course, mentally and spiritually.

Νέα Χώρα

Conversion Charts

Metric and Imperial Conversions
(These conversions are rounded for convenience)

Ingredient	Cups/Tablespoons/Teaspoons	Ounces	Grams/Milliliters
Butter	1 cup/ 16 tablespoons/ 2 sticks	8 ounces	230 grams
Cheese, shredded	1 cup	4 ounces	110 grams
Cream cheese	1 tablespoon	0.5 ounce	14.5 grams
Cornstarch	1 tablespoon	0.3 ounce	8 grams
Flour, all-purpose	1 cup/1 tablespoon	4.5 ounces/0.3 ounce	125 grams/8 grams
Flour, whole wheat	1 cup	4 ounces	120 grams
Fruit, dried	1 cup	4 ounces	120 grams
Fruits or veggies, chopped	1 cup	5 to 7 ounces	145 to 200 grams
Fruits or veggies, pureed	1 cup	8.5 ounces	245 grams
Honey, maple syrup, or corn syrup	1 tablespoon	0.75 ounce	20 grams
Liquids: cream, milk, water, or juice	1 cup	8 fluid ounces	240 milliliters
Oats	1 cup	5.5 ounces	150 grams
Salt	1 teaspoon	0.2 ounce	6 grams
Spices: cinnamon, cloves, ginger, or nutmeg (ground)	1 teaspoon	0.2 ounce	5 milliliters
Sugar, brown, firmly packed	1 cup	7 ounces	200 grams
Sugar, white	1 cup/1 tablespoon	7 ounces/0.5 ounce	200 grams/12.5 grams
Vanilla extract	1 teaspoon	0.2 ounce	4 grams

Oven Temperatures

Fahrenheit	Celsius	Gas Mark
225°	110°	¼
250°	120°	½
275°	140°	1
300°	150°	2
325°	160°	3
350°	180°	4
375°	190°	5
400°	200°	6
425°	220°	7
450°	230°	8

For conventional ovens, increase the baking length of time by about 25% and oven temperature by 25°F.